Advance Praise for *The Future of You* …

"*The Future of You* asks the question: 'But can you really begin to have a discussion about wealth if it ignores a significant part of what you value in your life?'

"The answer of course is *no*, what with all the harm that will otherwise ensue to those you love the most, your true wealth. The authors then offer the ways and means to discover your values and then how to create the collaborative team of advisors needed to put your answers into practice in your planning.

"Within this book's covers lies the combined wisdom of more than 600 years of experience in helping individuals clarify where their lives and their wealth intersect. Take the wisdom and use it to do the same for you and for those you love."

—James E. Hughes, Jr., author of
Family Wealth: Keeping It in the Family

"This exceptional book provides a roadmap that allows individuals and families to truly root their financial plans in the life footprints they are leaving or ultimately want to leave behind. Whereas most planning involves decisions around implementing various products and strategies to achieve the results, the authors of this book provide the insights to a more rewarding approach to effective decision-making that creates high-trust relationships, collaborating toward *The Future of You.*"

—Charles H. Green, co-author of
The Trusted Advisor and author of *Trust-Based Selling*

"This book makes the compelling case that true wealth, sustainable family and legacy wealth, flows from a deep understanding of one's authentic life purpose.

"The collaboration among the leading thinkers and wealth practitioners who contributed to this book offers comfort and clarity to everyone who is disconnected, confused, and overwhelmed by his or her relationship to money. Putting the "why" before the "how" is what makes its authors rock stars of the advisory world. After you devour the last page, seek them out—reach out and begin your own process of discovery."

—Tom Deans, Ph.D., best-selling author of
Every Family's Business

The Future of You

Providing Clarity Where Life Intersects Wealth

The Legacy Wealth Coach Network™

THE LEGACY WEALTH COACH NETWORK
NORTH AMERICA

Paperback 978-0-9851162-0-0
Hard cover 978-0-9851162-1-7
ebook 978-0-9851162-2-4

Printed in the United States of America
Edited by Jocelyn Baker (www.jocelynbakereditor.com)
Book design by Dotti Albertine (www.albertinebookdesign.com)

This book is dedicated to Scott Fithian (1961-2006),
whose amazing vision and unwavering passion
laid the foundation for the body of work represented in this book.

Although you passed long before your time,
your legacy carries on strong.

It is also dedicated to the members of
the Legacy Wealth Coach Network,
an incredible community of men and women
whose desire to advise clients through a process of
discovering their ultimate journey
shaped the pages of this book.

CONTENTS

Acknowledgments   *ix*

Foreword by Jim Stovall   *xi*

Introduction by Todd Fithian   *xv*

CHAPTER 1 Cutting Through the Noise   1

CHAPTER 2 Getting What You Want: The Power of Effective
           Decision-Making   13

CHAPTER 3 The Uncovering: Have You Had a Good Listening-To?   33

CHAPTER 4 Your Number: What Does It Mean?   47

CHAPTER 5 Wealth: Is It All About the Money?   63

CHAPTER 6 Your Footprints…Your Legacy   77

CHAPTER 7 Building Your Team   89

CHAPTER 8 Teamwork: Pulling in the Same Direction   99

CHAPTER 9 Are You Really Done?   111

A Note from Todd Fithian   *121*

Meet the Authors   *123*

ACKNOWLEDGMENTS

So many people have influenced the authors' thinking over the years that it would be extremely difficult to mention everyone, but we hope you know who you are.

Thank you to our dear friend, teacher, and mentor: Dr. Paul Schervish. You have forever changed our definition of wealth and provided us the confidence and the skills to lead a different conversation with our clients.

Thank you to the 19 brave advisors who teamed up on this project as the community of authors: William A. Barill, Daniel Barill, Mayur T. Dalal, John M. Dankovich, Chuck Ebersole, W. Duke Grkovic, Denice Gustin-Piazza, Scott D.C. Harris, Thomas P. Holland, Scott R. Lebin, Lawrence M. Lehmann, Allison Maher, Patrick O'Connor, Ed Postrozny, Tony A. Rose, Tom Sorge, Frank Spezzano, Robert Taylor, and Julianne Thornton.

We said from the beginning it wouldn't be easy, but the finished product is well worth the effort. As you know, this was a true collaboration and we are sure you can hear parts of your voices in the pages of *The Future of You.*

Thank you to our long list of advanced readers: George Arangio, Curt Fithian, Dennis Pawley, Kevin Sheard, Tim Belber, Shawn Postoff, Dana Mitchell, Don Wilson, Dashka Roth Lehmann, Rene Lehmann, Mr. and Mrs. Larry Dodds, Mr. and Mrs. Bob Carmen, Dr. and Mrs. Steve Fisher, Barbara Lebin, Elfrena Foord, Jim McEvoy, Nancy Hite, Eldridge Blanton, III, and Keith Berger.

We are forever grateful and appreciative for the time you gave to review our manuscript and the tremendous insights and advice that helped shape the final pages of this book.

Thank you to Jocelyn Baker, our amazingly talented editor. We are sure working with 19 authors sounded like a good idea when we started! You demonstrated amazing patience and helped us through the navigation of finding our voice in *The Future of You*!

Finally, special thank-you to the editorial committee members. You spent countless hours on the creation of this book. Sometimes you shared your thoughts, and sometimes you debated your views, and it was always powerful to watch you align your thinking. We will miss working together. The good news, though, is that our Friday morning 10 a.m. slot is now free! Congratulations for seeing the dream through to fruition and coordinating *The Future of You.*

John M. Dankovich
Chuck Ebersole
Todd A. Fithian
Lawrence M. Lehmann
Scott R. Lebin

by Jim Stovall, author of *The Ultimate Gift*

I have had the privilege of viewing wealth from the perspective of a very poor person as well as a financially independent person. I would be the first to say that money, in and of itself, does not make us happy. I would hasten to add that poverty does not make us happy either. All other things being equal, rich is better.

So what is the connection between money and happiness?

One of my first ventures was as an investment broker. I found that managing money came somewhat naturally to me, but the relationship between my clients and their money required deeper discovery. Mine was a "relationship business." I noticed that many—if not most—advisors struggled with that aspect. They spent all day analyzing markets, but conducting a meeting with the sole focus on their client's goals was somehow foreign. This early observation shaped my view of financial and estate planning. After all, I had several hundred clients, all of whom had different goals, dreams, and ambitions they expected their money to fulfill. How could I serve them by ignoring the "relationship" aspect of the business?

Though I had observed the hole in the financial-planning process, I still could not draw the connection between money and happiness. Prior to meeting my friends and colleagues in the Legacy Wealth Coach Network, my thoughts about money could be summarized in six words: *More is always better than less.*

Then I met Todd and Scott Fithian, founders of the Legacy Wealth Coach Network. The Fithians, along with several members of their network, and I collaborated on turning one of my books, *The Ultimate Gift,* into a major motion picture. *The Ultimate Gift,* along with the sequel book and movie, *The Ultimate Life,* successfully created a conversation about issues of money, wealth, and legacy.

When I wrote these books, my focus was not on the financial aspect of the stories. Instead, I focused on why parents and grandparents—regardless of financial resources—want to pass along their values to younger generations.

The authors of this book, all advisors within the Legacy Wealth Coach Network, trained me to make the connection between valuables and values. They taught me that passing on valuables without attaching them to values is ill-advised and even dangerous. The more attached a person's values are to his or her valuables, the more likely the person is to achieve happiness.

I ask readers to think about the list of things that are really important to them in a lasting and meaningful way. Likely, they will think of family, friends, health, faith, career passions, education, and the like. Money will probably not be on the list. Certainly, it will not top the list. Yet money is involved in every area of their lives. Nothing can take the place of money as a vehicle that allows individuals to procure the elements that are necessary for them to focus on and maintain the truly important things in their lives. How can they enjoy their families and friends unless they have money to put a roof over their head? How can they maintain their health without spending money to visit doctors, join gyms, or buy healthy food?

Money alone is not enough. What would people do with all the money in the world if they had no family or friends, poor health, and no sense of productivity? Would they simply roll around in a wad of cash?

Indeed, values and valuables are inseparable, yet the relationship between the two is often too shallow. Money is not often intentionally attached to values.

In *The Ultimate Gift,* a very wealthy man dies, leaving behind a spoiled, ungrateful grandson who expects to inherit the wealthy man's fortune. Unless this money is attached to values—such as gratitude, family, education, laughter, and dreams—the money will only serve to make the grandson even more unappreciative, entitled, and lazy.

Now let's make this personal. You likely can afford to send your children to the best schools, but how useful will this education be if your children are not taught respect, productivity, compassion, and good citizenship? Wealth can buy an education, but it alone cannot buy values.

The Legacy Wealth Coach Network made another important distinction regarding values and valuables: There is no one-size-fits-all solution. Over the last decade, I have read numerous books on financial and estate planning. Too many of these resources attempt to provide a universal solution. This book explains that there is no universal solution to financial and estate planning.

There *is* a universal truth. The universal truth is this: Your values are a critical component of your estate plan or financial plan.

My late, great friend, Scott Fithian, was fond of saying, "If you can tell a good story, you earn the right to share your message." The professionals who have been instrumental in compiling this book are unique in that they understand that the only story that really matters is yours.

As someone diagnosed early with a disease that would result in blindness, I was forced at a young age to consider the obstacles I would have in gaining employment, finding security, and simply navigating my day-to-day activities.

Eventually, I decided that if I carefully arranged a room in my house, I could create a safe place where everything was predictable and under control. I couldn't see to steer the ship, but I could operate out of this room forever.

Imagine what this was like. I was protected, but I was limited to activities that could be accomplished in a single room. I ran my business, made phone calls, and avoided embarrassing situations related to my blindness, but I lived my life in a 9 x 12 room.

I was finally able to leave this room because I was surrounded with people who believed that we are all giants in control of our destiny—people like the Fithians and the members of the Legacy Wealth Coach Network. I went on to become a national champion Olympic weightlifter, and an International Humanitarian of the Year, a tremendous honor considering the amazing list of people who have been bestowed this award. I have made movies and television accessible for America's 13 million blind and visually impaired people and their families through my Narrative Television Network.

I might be unable to see, but I can still steer my ship. As you begin your own financial and legacy journey through the pages of this book, remember that you should always be the one steering your ship. The people who have come together to make this book possible are simply along to help you discover and then navigate the course you have set. You will provide the answers—answers set in your values and attached to your valuables. The authors will ask the questions.

INTRODUCTION

by Todd Fithian, Managing Partner of The Legacy Companies,
co-author of *The Right Side of the Table*

Have you ever thought—and I mean really thought—about the purpose and mission of your own existence? Life has so much potential, yet we rarely take the time to reflect on the many shapes and sizes our life can take.

This book has been written to challenge the norm. You will reconsider your approach to planning, to the purpose and mission of your existence, and to your legacy. In this space, no right or wrong answers exist. However you define yourself—as a leader, a good man, a mom, a brother or a sister, a friend, an investor, a philanthropist, peacemaker, or whatever it might be—the pages of this book will help you begin your journey, showing you that you alone have the answers to your life questions.

We have not written this book as a self-help book, but as a catalyst for clarifying what is possible. If you think about your greatest accomplishments to date, I imagine that you, like others, did not achieve them on your own. Kurt Godel's Nobel-Prize-winning *Incompleteness Theorem* proved that we cannot reach success alone. A teacher, coach, parent, sibling, boss, mentor, clergyman, or perhaps a team of people, always helps along the way.

This book, as well as the Wealth Optimization System we present herein, is your next helper. You will be guided through a journey of possibilities in the realm of discovering your dreams and aspirations. At the same time, we will plug holes in your current plan. Our hope is that by the time you have finished reading, you will have discovered what you want for yourself. You will no longer be satisfied with the default plan; instead, you will be taking action toward the creation of your plan!

In 1995, I decided to join my brother Scott in business, to build the model for what a wealth-advisory practice should be. As third-generation financial advisors, we were clear that we wanted to build our business differently from our predecessors. Although our predecessors were successful, the model always required the sale of manufactured products—such as insurance or investments—for the advisor to be paid.

We struggled with this process. How could we objectively serve our clients when these products were the only recipes for success?

One day, Scott told me something that still gives me goose bumps today.

"Todd, we are going to change the industry model for how advisors work with their clients," he said to me. "We are going to build a model that doesn't yet exist."

For the next year, we traveled North America looking at all the client/advisor models out there, hoping to draw inspiration from another model. We came back empty-handed after each and every trip.

At the same time, we began conducting research by interviewing our clients. The results were staggering. Although our clients liked us on a personal level, they really didn't understand or appreciate our business model.

One of the clients who had purchased a product from us said, quite frankly, "We bought this simply because we wanted the process to stop. You must have visited us 17 times. We shudder to think of what you paid in gas alone, and since we weren't paying for your time, we figured the only way to compensate you for all your work was to buy something."

As we met with new clients, we found that this trend is pervasive in the traditional financial-planning approach. Have you ever felt pressured into buying a product? Maybe you still feel this way today.

Needless to say, such stories were exactly the confirmation we needed for the development of the Wealth Optimization System®.

In early 1997, we had a humbling experience. Scott and I had just returned from an industry meeting where we were asked to present our new client-centered business model to a group of our peers when the phone rang. On the other end was an advisor we had known for years.

He told us that he had a very important question for us: "Will you teach us?"

The next words that came out of his mouth changed our lives forever. He said: "A group of us got together after your presentation because we were so moved. We want to learn your process."

Scott and I—along with a good friend, colleague, and contributor to this body of work, Dr. Paul Schervish, the director at the Center on Wealth and Philanthropy and professor of sociology at Boston College—took them up on the offer.

Over a decade later, here sits the Legacy Wealth Coach Network to share our message. This book represents the work Scott, Paul, and I did, as well as contributions from the advisors who joined us on that journey, adding their own insights and invaluable approaches to planning.

The collaboration of authors who came together to share their wisdom, knowledge, and firsthand experience through this book, make it truly unique. The authors represent both the United States and Canada. They are accomplished wealth managers, financial advisors, accountants, insurance professionals, lawyers, and investment managers.

Together, we have brought more than 600 years of collective experience to the pages of this book. Though each of us has a different area of expertise, we share a common application of a process that allows you to make confident, enthusiastic decisions.

As you read through the pages of this book, you will appreciate how our discussions with clients are very different from the traditional conversations. We live in a solution-driven society where people want answers and results. In this book, you will learn that focusing on solutions is expensive and useless.

By placing your focus elsewhere, you will learn that the solution will almost fall into place. You will learn that your life will be richer as a result.

On September 4, 2006, Scott lost his long and hard-fought battle with pancreatic cancer. He had turned forty-five just seven days earlier. The stories and experiences shared through the chapters of this book are a fitting contribution to my brother's legacy.

Scott started his journey by defining his purpose and mission in life. He wanted to change the industry model for how advisors work with their clients. This book represents his life's work, and he would be proud to have it shared through the voices of these contributing authors with whom we have worked so closely over the years. Take a lesson from Scott and think about your purpose and mission. The opportunities are endless.

What's stopping you from starting your journey today?

CHAPTER 1

Cutting Through the Noise

Tom[1] cannot sleep.

In fact, Tom has been unable to sleep since his younger brother died. A few months ago, 59-year-old Gary kissed his wife good-bye, walked outside, and had a heart attack. An avid hiker and swimmer with no vices, Gary was in better shape than most 25-year-olds. Everyone expected him to recover.

He didn't.

Ever since that day, Tom's mind has been racing. He worries about his wife, his grandson, his business, his charities, his outdated estate plan, and his health. He worries about his money, his life insurance (or lack thereof), his business succession plan, the managers in his firm, his home, his son's many girlfriends, his teenage daughter, and his adult daughter—will she ever settle down and start her own family?

The more Tom worries, the more he tosses and turns.

We are bombarded.

Whether watching TV, listening to the radio, surfing the Net, watching previews, or pumping gas, we are constantly pitched, screamed at, belittled

---

1 Let's face it: Most people find the topic of wealth-planning to be dry. We tend to agree, so we are illustrating our point by following Tom and his family. We assure you that Tom and his family members are not actual people. Rather, their stories are used throughout this book to provide a concrete example and keep our readers engaged.

by, and confronted with product advertisements and promotions promising to improve our lives immeasurably.

This is just to stop dandruff!

To help us get rich, the ads and pitch people are not nearly as subtle. By the end of the day, we are beaten. When we go to bed, we do not count sheep; we count the tasks we have left undone, the money we have lost, and the opportunities seized by someone else.

What should we do? What should we buy? What should we invest and where? Whom should we trust with our money?

Our minds are buzzing with so much noise that we cannot simply stop, ponder, and make a decision.

WARNING

Skipping the foreword and introduction may cause confusion!

Statistically speaking, most people don't read the foreword and the introduction, jumping right in at Chapter 1. We caution this approach. You'll understand our process much better if you read these sections.

In response to this sensory assault, your selective listening abilities have evolved. Consider something as simple as watching the news. This experience has changed drastically over the past 30 years. To focus on the news, you must train your brain to ignore the information scrolling across the bottom of the screen. You must ignore the station logo that remains onscreen throughout the broadcast. You must also ignore your children, who are each having their own cell-phone conversations. In short, you must ignore the noise, selectively listening only to the significant information.

This is just one microcosm of your buzzing world. Google the phrase "wealth planning" and you will receive about nine million results. Try "financial planning" and you will get about 127 million results. Research any topic that comes to mind, and you will instantly access hundreds or thousands of solutions associated with a particular problem.

All these solutions might seem like great resources, but this unlimited access to information is just one more source of noise. With 127 million websites all promising to help you achieve your financial goals, how can you choose which one option is best?

It is easy to see why so many people are stuck in a realm of eternal planning, sorting through all the noise to find the relevant information. In addition, if you couple access to information with the scandals that have rocked the wealth-planning industry, it is no wonder that some clients choose to do nothing.

Though you are wired to respond to sensory overload, the noises that surround you have an insidious impact on your life, often stopping you from moving forward. You must recognize how this noise affects your decision-making abilities so that you can develop a coping process and avoid unintended consequences. The purpose of this chapter is to help you identify and ignore the products and messages that are simply making noise. Later on, this ability to cut through the noise will allow you to focus on your mission, vision, values, and goals so that you can have the necessary clarity to plan your future.

— THE SOURCE OF THE NOISE —

The traditional approach to planning involves three elements:

1. Gather data and identify goals.
2. Outline solutions to reach those goals.
3. Implement those solutions.

This process seems straightforward, but it misses a huge component: goal clarification. Sure, the traditional process relies on a generic "fact-finding" questionnaire, but this form usually serves as the only method of identifying a person's goals.

Unfortunately, this level of goal identification provides only a tenuous link between a client's goals and an advisor's solutions. When it comes to estate-planning, business-planning, or decision-making in general, the process often stalls because clients do not have a deep understanding of their goals. As a result, they lack a significant attachment to the solutions.

In their haste to provide solutions, advisors fail to dig deeply to find clients' most compelling goals. Clients are left feeling as though they should take action. However, they do not want to take action because the goals are simply not inspirational.

Let us make something clear. We certainly do not intend to communicate that advisors are a lousy bunch of scoundrels. Nothing could be further from the truth. After all, the authors of this book are all advisors, in some capacity or another. As a group of people, advisors are well-intentioned and are pleased when clients meet their goals and thrive.

The problem is not with advisors *per se*. Rather, the culture of the traditional planning process leaves little room for advisors to extract the pertinent information from clients, who have been conditioned to find a quick fix and have little patience for examining their personal life goals. Advisors, hungry to keep their clients happy, do not force the issue.

As a result, the very people to whom clients turn for help—advisors—cannot provide solutions that resonate. In their haste to provide a solution (any solution!), advisors simply create more noise.

Imagine your response to advice that is not based on deep and compelling goals. The noise can become deafening. *The advisor is an expert,* you think, *but his advice doesn't make any sense. It must be me. I must be missing something.* Your brain then starts swimming with all your different questions, concerns, and fears.

The truth, though, is that the advisor's input is often noise that you should be ignoring. The advisor is offering a river when you need a glass of water.

Tom had always pushed estate, financial, and legacy-planning issues to the back burner. Now Tom knows that he must act—and act fast—to make sure plans are in place to care for his family.

Tom has no idea where to start, but he knows that one of his biggest concerns is the welfare of his 13-year-old daughter, Kelly. Does he have enough assets to provide for Kelly in the event that he and/or his wife die or become disabled?

Tom is confused by all the commercials advertising different investment programs. Investment House A says it will guide him along the right path, whatever that is. Investment House B trumpets that it has answers to his questions!

(Of course, these are the same investment houses that assured him in 2007 that the economy would continue to grow. In fact, both Investment

House A and Investment House B said they could forecast probable outcomes with 95-percent confidence.)

Looking for a referral, he turns to his friends, his accountant, and his lawyer.

He finally decides on Andrew, an enthusiastic financial advisor licensed to sell securities, handle investment portfolios, and sell life insurance and annuities. Andrew is a one-stop shop.

Tom and Andrew have instant rapport when they meet early on a Thursday afternoon. Tom brings last year's tax return and a questionnaire he previously filled out detailing personal information, such as the age of his children and his financial holdings (his net worth is $8.7 million).[2]

He briefly tells Andrew about his family.

Tom (60) is married to Paula, his second wife. Together, Tom and Paula have a 13-year-old daughter, Kelly. Tom also has two children

---

2 Your personal net worth might be more or less than Tom and Paula's net worth, but as we have cited from the beginning, this book is not about the amount of money you accumulate. This book, as well as the successful planning process it advocates, are about reaching decisions to create the legacy you desire.

from his first marriage: Laura is 32 and single; Evan is 29, divorced, and father to four-year-old Jackson.

Tom is a partner in a business-consulting firm and has a retirement plan worth $1.5 million and investment assets worth $1 million. Jointly, he and Paula have an additional $1 million and no debt. Their home is valued at $800,000, and they own a $400,000 vacation home in the Florida Keys, where they expect to retire.

Paula is a teacher and plans to retire alongside her husband in five years. Her pension will provide an income of $40,000 per year.

"So what brings you here today?" asks Andrew.

"Well, I'm not sure," says Tom. He explains that although he has accumulated wealth, Tom is concerned about his family. He isn't sure how much money he needs so that he can be financially independent for the rest of his life, nor is he sure how to structure any remaining assets (will there be remaining assets?). He wants to make sure that Paula, Kelly, and his grandson, Jackson, have suitable financial reserves in the event of his death. He would like to leave his older children, Evan and Laura, sufficient funds to provide flexibility but not so much that they can live off of his assets.

Looking thoughtful, Andrew considers Tom's situation for a few minutes and declares that he has the solution for Tom and his family. He suggests using a $500,000 life-insurance policy with waiver-of-premium rider. The policy has a high cash-value buildup with a lower death benefit in order to promote more equity in the policy. He also suggests that Tom meet with an estate-planning lawyer to discuss drafting a will. Andrew's sincere and well-intentioned suggestion is designed to bring Tom security.

As Tom listens to Andrew, his mind starts spinning with questions: *A waiver-of-premium rider? High cash-value buildup? What does this mean?*

Still, Andrew sounds confident, and Tom thinks that life insurance is probably a good idea, so he returns home to tell Paula that he has found a solution that protects Kelly in the event of their death or disability.

A few days later, Tom receives a life-insurance application in the mail from Andrew, along with a note saying that both he and Paula should sign the documents. Andrew includes a prepaid Next-Day return envelope.

The envelope sits on Tom and Paula's kitchen counter for three weeks, during which time Andrew leaves several messages. Tom returns his calls once or twice to explain that he has not had the time to review and sign the documents that would establish the life-insurance policy.

What factors underlie this type of behavior? Why do so many people fail to follow through with recommended solutions?

Holly Green, a management consultant and former president of the Peter Blanchard Organization, has a theory about this. Green believes that advisors use a filter to view clients' lives. This filter is based on the advisors' perspectives, values, and history.

As a result, an advisor like Andrew might really like a technique. Andrew's own goals might be satisfied through a life-insurance policy. Because Andrew wants to respect Tom's time, he skips over clarity planning and instead logically concludes that all of his clients should adopt a life-insurance policy as a strategy for reaching their goals.

Because the clients feel little connection to the solution, they simply don't take action.

If Andrew were afforded the time to take a step back and review Tom's goals, he would realize that he has made an understandable but critical mistake. In the absence of another filter (Tom's and Paula's!), Andrew imposes his own plan on Tom and Paula. The life-insurance policy is not appropriate for Tom for a variety of reasons.[3]

Unfortunately, such plans are just more noise, causing Tom and Paula to tune out.

When engaged in the planning process, would it not be preferable to adopt a plan for you? For a plan to be successful, you must feel intimately connected to it. You must know where the plan is taking you. First and foremost, you must be able to cut through all the noise so that you and your advisor can clearly see your goals. This is what is meant by *clarity*. You must begin with the end in mind.

If you do not have confidence that your goals will be accomplished,

---

3 The policy would not provide enough death benefit for Tom and his family. The high cash-value buildup would not correspond to his family's needs and would cause the premium to be higher than necessary for a higher death benefit. The waiver-of-premium rider on the policy would not provide the security in the event of Tom's disability.

your Next-Day return envelope will sit on the kitchen counter for three weeks. Three weeks will become three months, which quickly will turn into a year. Lack of clarity leads to mistrust, and the process simply breaks down. The only thing that does get signed is the check you pay for a strategy you do not ultimately adopt.

Very few advisors feel comfortable taking the time to engage a client and uncover everything germane to the overall goal. The good news is that a client can find an advisor who does engage in clarity planning, although it is not easy. Simply outlining your expectations to the advisor is ineffective for two reasons. First, most people (including some advisors) are not good listeners. Even those advisors who are great listeners are not trained to focus on values and goals. Sure, they are told to focus on values and goals, but this is not the same thing as being trained.

When an advisor focuses on why a solution is appropriate or inappropriate for a particular client, the client suddenly feels comfortable and connected to the solutions. Rather than being inundated with lingo, products, and technical terms, the client is making decisions that have everything to do with the values behind the goals.

Herein lies another issue: People are often unclear about their values. They may have a gut feeling, but many clients have a difficult time articulating why they react to things in a particular way. Tom, for instance, felt the amount of life-insurance death benefit was not enough, but based on the premium for Andrew's recommended plan, Tom could not afford more. Tom could not articulate why he had this feeling because he was not yet crystal-clear about his values.

Imagine engaging a process that excels at extracting values. Clearly understanding both the why and the subsequent goals prompts quick action. Only when trained advisors focus on uncovering a client's values and goals do they have the context in which to make appropriate long-term recommendations. Focusing on why you have a certain goal and what you are trying to achieve in the long term ensures that you are clear about your long-term goals before a course of action is suggested.

No one knows the importance of the *why* better than the Cheshire Cat.

```
"Which road should I take?"
      Alice asked the Cat.
"Where do you want to get to?"
      the Cat asked helpfully.
"I don't know," admitted Alice.
   "Then," advised the Cat,
"any road will take you there."
```

The Cat is sending Alice an important message: If you do not know where you want to end up, it doesn't matter what you do. You are liable to reach someone else's goals, but you will never reach your own goals.

— KEY POINTS —

> With so much access to information, clients find it difficult to cut through the noise.

- Which information is relevant?

- What information should be ignored?

Unable to answer these questions, many clients simply choose to do nothing.

> When it comes to important business, family, financial, or legal decisions, a client must have a tremendous amount of clarity about why he or she is implementing a solution. If a client fails to feel a strong connection between his or her goals and the advisor's solutions, the client likely will not take action.

> When the advisor makes a recommendation about a solution before completely understanding the client's needs, the end result may be unfavorable: The client will not implement the recommendation.

> A client must find an advisor who wants and is able to take the time to clarify his or her mission, vision, values, and goals.

In doing so, the advisor will provide relevant solutions, and the client will cut through the noise, focus on applicable solutions only, and feel deeply connected to financial, business, estate, or family plans. The client, therefore, is more likely to take action.

> ❯ This book provides the system that allows the client and the advisor to gain clarity and implement relevant solutions so that the client can achieve and manage his or her goals.

CHAPTER 2

Getting What You Want:
The Power of Effective Decision-Making

Tom is frustrated. For some reason, his meeting with Andrew seemed a complete waste of time. He cannot pinpoint why he is failing to take action, but he feels angry—at himself and at Andrew. He desperately wants to accomplish at least some of his planning needs before the summer ends. He feels out of control and, unless he starts checking things off his list, he worries that he will never accomplish his goals.

So when Evan, his son, sends Tom an email asking if he can bring his latest girlfriend, Trish, to a family dinner, Tom's patience is tested. Ever since his divorce, Evan has had a string of relationships with questionable women. Tom strongly disapproves. Evan's girlfriends are usually unemployed, uneducated, and otherwise unappealing.

So without thinking, Tom responds: *That depends. Does she have a job?*

Of course, Tom cringes the minute he pushes "Send." *Should I have sent that?* Tom asks himself.

On the one hand, Tom is tired of sitting next to Evan's girlfriends during family dinner and listening to their idle banter. He is tired of plastering on a fake smile.

On the other hand, Evan is a grown man; Tom knows he should treat his adult son's relationships with respect.

When Evan receives the email, he feels his father's disapproval. Feeling angry and insulted, he carefully considers his response. Evan knows that his dad disapproves of his relationships, but Evan disapproved of Paula when she first married Tom, and he still treated her with respect (most of the time). Why can't his dad show the same courtesy and be polite about Evan's girlfriend?

After drafting a few responses, he finally settles on opting out: *Never mind, Dad. Trish and I will catch a movie that night instead.*

Now no one is getting what he wants. Evan does not get to introduce his girlfriend to his father. Tom, who is trying to bring his family closer together, does not get to have dinner with his son.

Perhaps this analogy[4] seems a little juvenile, but haven't we all regretted sending an email the minute we push "Send"? Have we not all spouted off a minute too soon and embarrassed ourselves, caused friction, or ended a relationship that could have been saved?

This often happens because we do not begin with the end in mind. Tom and Evan's emails are an analogy for what can happen in a financial situation—and in life—if we do not consider our mission and honor our values.

We all have values, and with every decision we make, we either honor or dishonor them. Yet most of us fail to identify values intentionally, which means we are more likely to dishonor them.

To identify and articulate values in the planning world, Wealth Coaches use a process called **Discovery**. Discovery is the process of beginning with the end in mind. Of course, having clarity about your finances is a step in the right direction, but beginning with the end in mind must include a broader thought process that also considers your overall mission, vision, values, and goals.

Discovery answers these questions:

- *What do I want my life to look like in future years?*
- *How would I like to be spending my time?*
- *How would I like to impact others?*
- *How do I want my legacy to be built and continued?*

---

4 Though this book, as well as the solution presented herein, is specific to financial strategies, we often use examples that are not related to finances for the sake of simplicity. We do this because financial issues become complex, particularly when products, industry terms, and asset structures are introduced. Therefore, we often opt for analogies that demonstrate a point without introducing financial jargon.

- *How can I align my financial resources with the goals I want to accomplish during my lifetime?*
- *How can I prioritize my top five or six values so that I can use them as a personal filtering system designed to foster good decisions and behaviors?*

Let's go back to the analogy of Tom and Evan. Let's say that Tom's top five values are:

1. Family
2. Integrity
3. Faith
4. Education
5. Productivity

Though he did not consciously consider his top value, Tom created "family dinner night" in response to this value. He wanted to bring his family closer together.

Because he had never articulated or prioritized his values, he pushed "Send" without making sure his actions were in line with his goals. Simply by contemplating his values, Tom might have crafted a response to Evan that honored his goal of bringing his family closer together. Consider how the situation might have played out.

When Evan sends Tom an email asking if he can bring his latest girlfriend to a family dinner, Tom's patience is tested. He is tired of plastering on a fake smile while he tries to connect with Evan's latest girlfriend. However, he also knows that his relationship with Evan has been strained ever since he married Paula, less than a year after his divorce was finalized from Evan and Laura's mother.

He doesn't want to cause any unnecessary tension, especially because he values his family first and foremost.

He crafts his email to Evan carefully.

Sure! Bring Trisha. Just one request: Can the two of you meet me for coffee tomorrow so I can get to know her a little before dinner on Saturday? Family dinner is the only opportunity I have all week to spend time with my entire family, and I don't want it to be awkward. I'd rather meet her ahead of time so that we are both comfortable with each other on Saturday.

Tom feels at ease when he pushes the "Send" button. He has honored his top value—family. Instead of doing something divisive, his email has articulated how valuable Evan is to his father.

Tom smiles when he sees Evan's response:

Sure, Dad. Does the corner coffee shop at 7:00 a.m. work for you? Sorry for the early hour, but you will be impressed—Trish has a job, so she will have to leave by 7:30. Love you, Evan.

Liken this story to a financial choice. By identifying your values, every decision you make can be filtered through your values before you push "Send"—that is, before you sign a contract, or agree to a strategy. When you follow your values, the decisions become easier to pinpoint and implement.

Briefly stated, examining your mission, vision, values, and goals creates a journey of clarity. Knowing where you have been and answering the question, "What is next?" enable you to form a clear vision of where you want to go.

Oh brother, you might be thinking. *This sounds pretty difficult to do. After all, I want planning, not a psychoanalytic discourse on my life!*

The reality is that many of us go through life lacking clear intention. Our behaviors are simply self-contained behaviors, void of any real meaning. Instead of being an integrated part of an overall plan, your activities exist as if on a list—ticked off one by one but without your having a true feeling of accomplishment.

Is your behavior tied to personal success in business? Is having a successful business even important to you? Maybe your behavior should be tied to being the best provider for your family—your business's success is simply a steppingstone to reaching this goal. Do you want to raise socially responsible children? Is sustaining a lifetime family unit important? If you do not have clarity about your mission and value, you cannot make appropriate choices in the many instances where life intersects wealth.

To be clear, life always intersects with money, regardless of your socio-economic status.

On the heels of a less-than-productive meeting with Andrew, Tom is dreading his meeting with Jennifer, an estate-planning lawyer highly recommended by Andrew. He has not updated his estate plan since he and his first wife divorced. His plan is outdated by 15 years, a second wife, a third child, and a first grandchild, not to mention the millions of dollars his business is now worth.

Tom expected to spend the meeting talking about the various will and trust structures he should immediately establish. Instead, he is taken aback with Jennifer's first set of questions.

"I'd like to start by asking you some questions that will help clarify your goals and help me better understand exactly what you envision for your future. For instance, are there any specific goals you'd like to see accomplished through our work together? If you can envision your ideal future, what would that look like—both personally and professionally?"

"You are going to be sitting there a long time if you want me to answer all those questions," says Tom with a laugh.

"Good," says Jennifer. "I need to know as much about your mission, vision, values, and goals as possible before I can recommend strategies."

Tom is surprised, to say the least. He had expected Jennifer to recommend a few strategies and then ask him to fill in some forms.

"Let's start here: When we talked on the phone, you said you couldn't sleep because of the anxiety around your future. What are some of the issues that are keeping you awake at night?"

Tom tells Jennifer that he is worried that his older children will never bond with his second wife and their younger sister. Barring some freak accident, he will probably die before his wife, who is a decade younger. Will Evan and Laura continue having a relationship with Paula and Kelly once Tom is gone?

"I know the answer to this might seem obvious, but I want to know in your words why it is important to you that your kids have a relationship," says Jennifer. "Can you share this with me?"

"My brother died recently," explains Tom, "and, while we had a great relationship, we had grown apart over the past few years. I regret the trips we didn't take together, the laughs we didn't share. I want my kids to have a bond similar to my bond with Gary. I don't want them ever to lose it."

"What are some of the resources that you have that will allow you to help your children bond with each other and with your wife?" asks Jennifer.

"They all love me and want me to be happy, so they make an effort," says Tom. "My grandson, Jackson, becomes the center of everyone's world when he's around, so I think Evan and Paula could bond through Jackson. I also get to spend a lot of time with my kids. We all live in the same city, and even my adult children spend at least one evening a week at the house."

"Okay, if you think we've covered all the resources, let's talk a little bit about your obstacles. What are the obstacles to achieving this goal?"

Tom thinks for a minute, and then says, "I guess there is just one big obstacle."

"Are they going to fight over my assets when I die? I hear horror stories about this. I have no idea what will happen to my assets when I die. If everything transfers directly to her, then I worry about what will happen when she dies. I want to put something in place so that I can make sure my children and grandchildren all receive a portion of my assets," he says.

"I think we just identified another one of your goals," says Jennifer. "You want to bring your family closer together, and you want to make sure your assets are structured properly. Does that clearly reflect what you're saying?"

"Absolutely," says Tom.

"If I could provide you with a solution so that we could begin working toward accomplishing those goals today, how would you rank those goals on a scale of 1 to 5, with 1 meaning you would like to get started today?" asks Jennifer.

"Probably a 2 or 3 on both," says Tom. 'I think I'm getting a little ahead of myself. I don't even know whether I have enough assets to last me until my death. I'm worried about what is going to happen after I retire."

He explains that he is approaching retirement age and is planning on selling his interest in the business. However, he isn't sure how much money he will need to make from the sale of his business to sustain his lifestyle and meet his legacy goals.

"I have three partners, all friends from college, so we are all approaching retirement age at the same time. We don't have a solid exit strategy in place, but we think we will have an opportunity for liquidity in the coming years. We estimate that each partner's share of the business is worth $4 million," Tom tells Jennifer.

"I'm not sure what we should do, though," Tom continues. "We have four senior associates who don't have an equity stake but who have expressed interest in buying the firm. The problem is that they have limited financial capacity. My partners and I aren't sure what we will do. We could try to find a creative strategy for passing the business to the younger managers, find an outside buyer, or attempt an Initial Public Offering."

As Tom continues to talk, Jennifer learns more and more about him.

Tom confesses that as much as he loves his work and his family, he feels a little empty. He doesn't feel as if he is doing anything that will make a lasting difference.

"Paula and I give generously to various causes, but all I do is sign a check, and it's important to me that I do a little more," Tom tells Jennifer.

"Why is this important?" she asks.

"I just don't feel fulfilled when I merely sign a check," he explains.

"Is there anything specific that would help you feel fulfilled?"

"I'd like to be more involved in something educational," he says. "My grandson, Jackson, attends this wonderful little Montessori school. Sometimes the school has Open House for family members, and I get to sit and watch as these kids discover the world simply by observing and manipulating the environment around them. My wife is a teacher. She's always telling me stories about what the kids are learning. It's really exciting to me."

"Speaking of your wife," interrupts Jennifer, "I think she should come in the next time we talk. I want to make sure that we are all on the same page, and it's very important to bring her voice into the discussion before we begin to make any decisions. It's really important that I'm clear about both your goals. We've made a lot of progress. The more we talk, the more I can refine my suggestions for you and your family. It sounds as if you have a lot on your plate, and you have a few existing gaps in your current plan that need to be addressed."

"What do you mean?" asks Tom.

"As you talk, I'm spotting some gaps in your planning knowledge," Jennifer says, explaining that he and his advisors need to know:

- The dollar amount that he needs to be financially independent.
- The source of his post-retirement income.
- How (and whether) his business will turn into an asset that will provide security for him in the future.

To close these gaps in knowledge, Jennifer suggests two strategies.

First, Jennifer suggests that they prepare a Financial Independence Assessment. This will determine and clarify the capital required to provide for his financial independence and the sources from which cash flow will be delivered.

At the same time, Jennifer suggests that Tom begin creating a Family Legacy Report. She explains that, among other things, a Family Legacy Report will assess the capital required to provide for Paula, Kelly, Evan, Laura, Jackson, and any other grandchildren (in varying ways). The Report will also help Tom reach his philanthropic goals.

The more Tom talks to Jennifer, the more excited he becomes. He realizes why he never signed the documents from Andrew. He just didn't have ownership of the strategy. Though Tom felt a bond with Andrew, the plan itself felt cold and impersonal.

Tom cannot wait to get the ball rolling. With Jennifer, Tom isn't just signing forms (and checks)—he is impacting his life and creating a legacy for his family. Rather than having an *impression* of Tom and his family, Jennifer was spending time trying to understand Tom and his family. As a result, Tom feels in control of the process and attached to it.

Welcome to the Wealth Optimization System, an exciting and powerful process that allows you to uncover your goals, honor your values, and pursue your life vision.

— THE WEALTH OPTIMIZATION SYSTEM® —

The Wealth Optimization System is designed to help a client achieve clarity by eliminating background noise and giving sharp focus to the client's mission, vision, values, and goals. Therefore, the Wealth Optimization System has a different starting point from traditional financial and estate planning models. Before you and your advisor decide on strategies, you must first discover your mission, vision, values, and goals. The specifics of these elements are your "why."

Wealth Coaches call this "above-the-line" planning. Only when we know *why* you are embarking on a planning process can we begin to determine how we can help you reach your goals. Once we enter into *how* territory, we begin looking at strategies, tactics, and tools. This is called "below-the-line" planning.

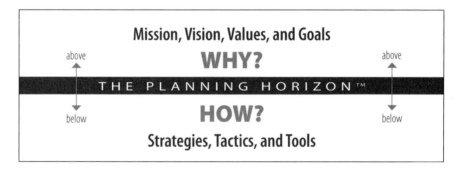

Unlike the traditional planning process, which spends most of the time "below the line," you and your advisor should spend most of your time "above the line."

Let's return to the analogy of Tom's pushing "Send" too early when responding to Evan's request to bring his girlfriend to family dinner. Tom originally spent all of his time "below the line." Instead of considering his values, he immediately decided on a strategy, pushing "Send" before he analyzed the end result. The strategy ended up dishonoring his values.

When Tom spent time "above the line" considering his values before he pushed "Send," his strategy was more appropriate. His son felt honored and respected, which meant that Tom strengthened his bond with his son.

Likewise, when Tom met with Andrew, the financial advisor, Andrew jumped immediately "below the line." As a result, Tom felt disengaged from the strategy because it was not connected to his values. When Tom met with Jennifer, the estate-planning lawyer, he spent the majority of his time "above the line." As a result, because he was gaining clarity, he was excited to move forward.

The Wealth Optimization System uses a specific four-part process to help you stay "above the line" long enough to discover your goals, traveling "below the line" only to create and implement appropriate solutions, then traveling back "above the line" to sustain, evaluate, and manage your desired results over time.

The Wealth Optimization System™

PHASE ONE: THE DISCOVERY PHASE

When was the last time you had a really good "listening-to"? Does your advisor ask you good questions and then keep quiet long enough to really listen to your answers, document your responses, honor your answers, and ask for clarification? When it comes to meeting with your financial advisor, you probably have not had a good "listening-to" since your first meeting.

The Discovery Phase is designed to help you gain clarity about what you want. This includes identifying your ideal vision for the future, as well as uncovering any related goals or obstacles that might affect your desired outcome. This process employs different approaches to guarantee that your true goals and objectives are rising to the surface. In other words, it causes you to think and allows you the opportunity to be heard.

Many clients can rattle off a quick answer about when they want to retire. When pressed to address *why* they want to retire, a much deeper discussion will ensue. This method of deep questioning is an important part of the Wealth Optimization System. Advisors help their clients reach clarity by searching for themes, challenging responses, identifying inconsistencies, and making sure that any contradictions are eliminated.

This process of deep questioning helps you identify all the reasons why you want to do something. This process is similar to an archeological dig: Each question helps you go deeper and deeper until clarity begins to emerge. Your financial advisor acts as your guide, navigating the pitfalls to take you on a safe journey.

**This Discovery Phase contains three elements:
PAST, PRESENT, and FUTURE.**

Begin by looking at your PAST. What decisions and planning have you completed to date? What motivated you to complete the plan you currently have? If you have not done any planning, what has prevented you from taking action? How are your values an outgrowth of your past experiences?

Next, focus on the PRESENT. In an ideal world, what would you like to have in place that has not been accomplished? What financial needs do you currently have? How clear are you regarding your current financial situation as it relates to your future needs? What are your values?

The third and final element in the Discovery Phase is taking the time to identify your FUTURE needs and goals. What do you want your future to look like? What do you want to be able to do so that you can live your ideal existence? Discovering that you do not have to be a victim of your past—that you can craft your own future and create your own life story—is an empowering realization included in this stage.

Upon first entering the Discovery Phase, many clients are concerned about the time it will take, but this questioning process does not add to the overall time it takes to complete and implement a plan. The goal of the Discovery Phase is to eliminate noise and clarify your individual needs. This process actually saves time because it makes the next stages easier to accomplish. Once you have reached clarity, you will have a new level of confidence. The "how" will become obvious because you will be clear on the "why."

Let's take a look at how Discovery works, using an intentionally oversimplified example.

Tom has been asked to contribute to his grandson Jackson's Montessori school. He has not yet decided whether donating or volunteering is the best way to make a difference at this school. He begins examining this by asking himself one question: *If I were to imagine the ideal future related to my selected need, what would that look like?*

Tom describes his ideal future with respect to Jackson's education: "I play an active role in Jackson's education. I know his teachers. I know about the projects on which he is working. I am deeply connected to his strengths and his interests. I use my experience to help him find opportunities my own children did not have. As a result, he has direction and focus throughout his education."

PHASE TWO: THE CREATIVE SOLUTIONS PHASE

Once you and your advisor have identified your goals, you will find the motivation and confidence to move "below the line" and enter the second phase. In the Creative Solutions Phase, you will consider appropriate solutions for the problems identified in the Discovery Phase. Therefore, these solutions are aligned with your mission, vision, values, and goals. The number of solutions available will be determined by what will best close the gap for your individual situation. In other words, the mission, vision, values, and goals you discovered while "above the line" will serve as your filter while "below the line."

This phase cannot begin until you have reached true clarity about the various goals and objectives. All too often, people tell us that they have been through a financial planning process before, so they don't need comprehensive planning. They will proudly show off the five-inch binder that contains this masterful plan. However, when asked about the actions they have taken, they have nothing to show. This doesn't mean that the plan in the binder was a bad plan. It does mean, however, that some of the solutions were not aligned with their mission, vision, values, and goals. It means that the clients never truly bought into and took ownership of the plan.

The advantage of spending sufficient time "above the line" becomes evident when you travel "below the line" into the Creative Solutions Phase. It becomes much easier to identify which strategies are appropriate and which are not. Although a solution might be legal, used by many people, or sold extensively by an advisor, it may not be appropriate when filtered through your family's mission, vision, values, and goals.

Solutions do not have to be complicated, but without worthwhile and meaningful experiences in the Discovery Phase, successful decisions cannot be made. The Creative Solutions Phase is often the place where you begin to take ownership of your strategy because you are clear about why each decision is being made. Clarity arising from a positive experience in the Discovery Phase will allow you to make decisions comfortably—perhaps for the first time in your life.

When deciding how he wants to contribute to Jackson's Montessori school, Tom considers several solutions:

Solution #1: He can afford to donate to the school, but this would not help him accomplish his goal of feeling deeply connected to the school.

Solution #2: Tom could volunteer at Jackson's school. This would certainly help him develop a close relationship with Jackson's education, but this might be difficult given his current schedule.

Solution #3: Tom could take part in after-school activities. Three times a year, the children perform a play or musical. Tom is handy and could help build sets; Paula is an expert seamstress and could help with costumes. Tom loves this idea. Not only would he be actively involved in the school, but he could also include Paula, which might bring Evan, Jackson, and Paula closer together.

Solution #4: Tom knows that the school desperately needs money. He could leverage his business skills to help raise funds for the school. Like Solution #3, this would also help him develop relationships with Jackson's teachers.

After measuring the solutions in relation to his values, Tom ranks the solutions as follows:

1. Fundraise
2. Build sets and sew costumes
3. Donate
4. Volunteer during school hours

PHASE THREE: THE STRATEGY DEPLOYMENT PHASE

After powerful experiences in the initial two phases, the Strategy Deployment Phase is the next logical step in the planning cycle. This phase is virtually stress-free because of the time spent in the first two phases.

In traditional approaches to planning, this stage usually presents the biggest hiccups. Many people spend their lives getting ready to get ready. They are always going to implement a plan tomorrow, but somehow they never get around to it. They fail to act because they are not convinced that what they are about to implement is in their best interest.

These people are stuck in eternal planning. They spend months or years looking at the various pros and cons of the many strategies available. They analyze every tactic and tool on the market, eventually feeling paralyzed by all the noise.

Deploying a decision is easy when it is part of an overall process. At this stage, if the strategy is aligned with your needs and accomplishes your goals, you will have no reason or desire to postpone implementation.

During the Strategy Deployment Phase, most people will have reached peace of mind. They know the next phase of the process—Results Management—will adjust for any changes that might occur and will manage the results of the strategy deployment. In this phase, clients understand that each step in the process is interconnected. They are not planning in a vacuum; rather, they are correlating and integrating each decision to achieve their overall mission, vision, values, and goals.

As a matter of practicality, Tom decides not to volunteer at Jackson's Montessori school during school hours. Though he would enjoy this, Tom knows that he would have to sacrifice other goals—namely, his career—to make this happen. At least until he retires, he will have to take a less active role in his grandson's education. He can fundraise, donate, and help with the school plays. His action steps are:

✓ Ask about the school's fundraising efforts. Who are the people involved? Is there a formal plan? Does the school have any slots left?

Tom learns that the fundraising committee consists of several businesswomen and men, including bankers and financial advisors. The committee's secretary recently retired from the role when his daughter graduated.

Tom immediately volunteers for the role.

✓ Ask about the school's set designers and seamstresses. He learns that a set designer is needed, and so is a seamstress. Paula—desperate for Evan's approval and enthusiastic about Jackson's education—eagerly volunteers, and the couple starts volunteering to help behind the scenes at school plays.

✓ Cut a check.

PHASE FOUR: THE RESULTS MANAGEMENT PHASE

In the words of Winston Churchill, "It's not the end. It's not even the beginning of the end, but it's the end of the beginning."

You have started the process, a process that will continue until each and every one of your goals has been met. You will find that this process will not only allow you to realize your goals, but it will also allow you to adjust them, build upon them, change them, and set new ones.

You do this by climbing back "above the line" again to test the results continuously for relevance and sustainability. Are the goals still relevant to your life? Here, you and your advisor will review the plan, making sure that you continue to be confident about the plan and connected to it.

The traditional model misses this commitment to regular monitoring and review and, of all the planning phases, this one is the most important. By committing to a schedule of reviewing and revisiting your mission, vision, values, and goals, you can continue to own your plan.

❖❖❖

Three months into Tom's volunteer work at the Montessori school, he takes a step back. He is thrilled with the amount of money he has helped the school raise. Using some of the same online marketing strategies his own company has used, Tom helped the school raise three times as much money as the year prior!

Tom develops some obstacles because the set design work is intense, and Tom is 60 years old. He has started having minor back pains, and he isn't sure he can withstand the physical pressure of continuing to build sets. Tom decides to search aggressively for a replacement.

Paula, on the other hand, loves being the school's seamstress, especially after one of the teachers commented that the costumes were the most beautiful the staff and students had ever seen!

— KEY POINTS —

> If we do not begin with the end in mind, we will miss the critical step of intentionally identifying values. As a result, we might make decisions that dishonor our values.

> When confronted with a problem or need, most people— advisors and clients alike—immediately begin seeking solutions instead of gaining clarity around the problem or need. Because these solutions are not filtered through a value system, the solutions are often inappropriate.

> The Wealth Optimization System uses a horizontal plane we call "The Planning Horizon" to explain this problem. Most people start "below the line" to consider strategies, tactics, and tools. Instead, they should start "above the line," first considering mission, vision, values, and goals.

> ❯ The Wealth Optimization System can be further divided by a vertical line to create a four-part process that forces clients and advisors to gain clarity first. Only upon identifying a vision and goals can the client and advisor move "below the line" to consider solutions and implement solutions. After briefly dipping "below the line," the client and advisor move "above the line" to manage the results, clarify goals, and refine the values.

CHAPTER 3

The Uncovering:
Have You Had a Good Listening-To?

Tom has ten hours to accomplish 24-hours'-worth of tasks. His head is swimming with the day's priorities, so when Paula asks him what time he will be home from work, he simply says, "Yes."

Kelly giggles, and asks, "Dad, can I borrow the car today?"

Tom hands his car keys to his 13-year-old daughter before he realizes that Kelly doesn't even have a driver's license.

"You got me," he laughs.

Tom turns to Paula, "Did I just say *yes* when you asked me what time I'd be home from work?"

Paula nods and raises an eyebrow.

"I guess I am not listening. I have a million things to do today. I will be home tonight at 7:00 and, Kelly, I will drop you off at school. You can choose the radio station, but I am holding onto the keys," he says, snatching them back from Kelly.

When Tom arrives at the office, his first call is to his financial advisor, Andrew. Tom still has not signed the life-insurance application Andrew sent and, after meeting with Jennifer, now he knows why he failed to take action.

Somewhere deep within, a tiny voice had been asserting itself. This niggling little voice was so quiet that it was inaudible to his conscious mind but, like *Horton and the Who,* Tom's subconscious mind heard it and stuck to its guns.

He lacked confidence about the plan drawn up by Andrew because Andrew's planning process did not involve a process whereby Tom was able to specify his goals. Furthermore, Tom could not understand how the proposed insurance would help his family's situation. Tom did not want to put his blind trust in a cookie-cutter plan that could work for most people most of the time. He wanted a complete and comprehensive plan that was painstakingly tailored to his family's unique circumstances and dreams.

Tom wants to explain his concerns to Andrew and give him a chance to rectify them.

"Tom!" Andrew says enthusiastically. "I am glad to hear from you. I have been worried about your insurance plan. We can't implement it until I receive the signed documents from you."

"I will be honest," says Tom. "I am not ready to sign those documents. I just do not think I have had a good listening-to."

On the other end of the line, Andrew listens. As he hears Tom's thoughts, he begins nodding enthusiastically.

True, a few advisors are in it just for the buck, but, like most financial advisors, Andrew really wants to see his clients succeed. Of course, he wants to make a living, but his passion is watching clients meet and exceed their financial goals.

Andrew knows that financial goals are just one part of the picture. He understands that money is only a tool to reach a goal. Unfortunately, most of his clients have little time to sit and explore their more meaningful life goals.

As a result, Andrew has always focused on money only. As he listens to Tom speak, he realizes that he finally has an opportunity to start focusing on the intersection of life goals and money.

For most of us, day-to-day tasks and activities tend to soak up our focus like thirsty sponges. Not only are we caught in the trap of feeling like we must be productive—actively doing something every moment of the day—but we also fail to dream.

Our busy schedules are augmenting another problem that inhibits our dreams from turning into reality. Most of us need someone who will listen to us and coach us. Burdened by distraction upon distraction, we simply do not have a process that forces us to slow down and intentionally create our own destinies.

That's right: We can create our own destinies.

Of course, this is easier said than done. To move from imagination to creation, we must have a process, as well as an advisor who attempts to uncover our deepest desires. The five steps of the VISOR model serve as this process, creating an environment for clients to discover their priorities, capacities, obstacles, and motivations.

Visioning and defining goals,
Prioritizing goals according to their **I**mportance,
Identifying **S**upporting resources,
Identifying **O**bstacles, and
Measuring **R**eadiness to move forward.

Going through this process helps you not only identify goals, but also determine which goals are lacking conviction or are superficial, and which ones are the true desires of your heart.

For most of us, this process is impossible to complete entirely on our own. We need someone who will listen to us. Having a trusted confidante who is committed to helping us define and manage our desired outcomes throughout the process is critical. This person can bring the lens of objectivity to our VISOR experience. After all, each of us has a unique point of reference limited by our own experience. We simply do not know what we do not know. Another person's perspective can challenge us to think outside of our own box.

Let us now take a look at each step of the VISOR process.

VISION

In the first chapter, you learned that most planning models have three steps:

1.   Gathering data and establishing goals,
2.   Outlining solutions to reach these goals, and
3.   Implementing those solutions.

Under the typical model, you and your advisor set goals, and you then busily go about trying to figure out ways to achieve those goals. Once you have the solution (which usually occurs during the same meeting as the goal-setting), you implement it.

We learned that many planning mechanisms are not implemented because the typical model fails to connect the plan to the client's deep and compelling goals. (Remember Tom's unsigned documents?)

The Wealth Optimization System considers goal-setting to be the beginning of a much more in-depth process. During the Discovery Phase, you must ask various questions about what you want. You must consider your vision from different points of view, such as your personal, business, family, spiritual, health, and financial goals.

We begin with one question: *What is the vision of your ideal future?*

If this question is the only thing you address upon reading this book, we will consider ourselves successful. Before attempting to achieve your goals, you must consider what will happen in your life when you do achieve them. Look into the future and imagine what every aspect of your life would be like. For instance:

- What would life be like within your family?
- How about your financial life or your involvement in your community?
- How might your physical health be affected?
- How would your spiritual life develop?

Tom, Jennifer, and Paula are in the middle of a long conversation about Tom and Paula's vision. Among other things, Tom and Paula have identified the following:

- He and Paula need to determine what level of financial independence would sustain their lifestyle and help them continue to pursue their values of family, integrity, faith, education, and productivity. Tom and Paula don't know what it means to be financially independent because Tom does not know how much money he needs in order to sustain his lifestyle until both he and Paula die.

- Tom wants to provide Paula with suitable financial resources in the event of his death or disability. Once again, Tom doesn't know what "suitable financial resources" means.

- Tom and Paula want to leave a lasting and meaningful legacy, which they have not yet defined.

- Tom wants to provide resources for Kelly and his grandson so that they are cared for until adulthood, including money to pay for high-quality educations.

- Tom wants to provide financial resources so that Laura and Evan—and Kelly and Jackson, once they reach adulthood—can take advantage of opportunities, but he doesn't want to leave so much that they will not have to work.

- Tom and Paula want the excess capital—whatever it might be—to provide for the community in which they live.

- Tom wants to have a business-succession plan, complete with all the documents necessary to sell the business.

- Paula wants to strengthen her relationship with Evan and Laura.

Once you have identified what your ideal life looks like, find a way to grab onto it so that you can become truly committed to it. Some people feel success, and are able to take a major step toward experiencing the power of desire and commitment. Others are able to intellectualize success, but might not "feel" it until the goal has been reached. Either approach is right, as long as it helps you increase your commitment to the goal.

When you can feel, visualize, or intellectualize the experience, you then have the spark that will drive you to achieve your goals. You have created a vision for your future. This vision is the most important part of the VISOR model. It will be used as the starting point to begin the planning process.

A trained advisor asks enough questions to extract a person's vision, making sure to clarify and pinpoint details, and question any conflicts. For instance, Jennifer might ask Tom: *Imagine you have a crystal ball and are looking into the future. If all of your dreams and goals have come true, can you describe what your life looks like?*

These questions inspire people to think about their future in specific, crystal-clear terms. Our objective is to move beyond the emotional topics and events of today and become immersed in visualizing a successful future. Beginning with the end in mind, we facilitate a discussion around a client's vision and goals.

Keep in mind that your vision must be updated regularly (see sidebar) and that you might have several different visions. The life you envision likely includes several different goals—some related and others totally unrelated. If you are a parent, you may have several goals that pertain to your children: to educate them, to pay for a wedding, or to give them an opportunity to travel abroad. You may also have goals around a hobby or passion, and still others pertaining to your career. These goals might or might not be related.

Remember that you must go through the VISOR process often.

In *Alice in Wonderland,* the caterpillar asks Alice: "Who are you?"

"I—I hardly know, sir, just at the present—at least," says Alice. "I know who I was when I got up this morning, but I think I must have been changed several times since then."

This is often how our past, present, and future lives can be viewed. We are not today who we were yesterday; after our conversations today, we will be changed tomorrow. We are continually creating and adjusting our vision of the future.

Because the vision drives the entire planning process, Wealth Coaches advise everyone—from first-time planners to multi-generational families to those who believe their planning is complete—to review their vision regularly. Because life changes, a person's mission, vision, values, and goals will change as well. Reviewing one's vision, and the planning done as a result, allows the client to make sure his or her plan remains relevant.

IMPORTANCE

As we noted earlier, you might have several different visions related to the different areas of your life. Clarifying the importance of your vision or visions will help you attach significance and prioritize all your different goals.

You will start this journey by asking one question: *Why is this vision so important to me?*

When Jennifer asks Tom and Paula why their goals are important to them, they rattle off several answers. Paula says:

> "I want to spend more of my time giving back to the community."

> "I want to make sure my daughter is taken care of through college, in the event something happens to us."

> "I need to know that my family understands and supports my goals."

> "I want to have a clear understanding of our financial goals, and whether we have enough money for the rest of our lives."

Tom adds to this:

> "I want to have more time to spend with Paula, my kids, and my grandson."

> "I want to know that my family is secure."

> "I need to know if I can afford to retire."

What is it about your vision that makes you feel so good? Would you like to take care of your family? Would you like to work in the community? Do you feel compelled to share your experiences? Is it because you want to spend more time with your family, or have an impact on your family by transferring your values to them?

In answering this question, you might find that a component of your vision is not important to you. This process helps you decide which goals you want to pursue, recognizing the costs and trade-offs associated with each of them.

For instance, Tom has always wanted to travel and become a "citizen of the world." With his retirement fast approaching, he will have the time and resources to turn this dream into a reality. How important is this goal if it means that he will be separated from his family? Considering the importance of a goal forces a person to determine whether a goal is worth pursuing.

Eventually, you should create a hierarchy of importance so that highest-priority goals can be achieved first. Examining the importance of your vision helps you reinforce the need to move forward and take action on the steps necessary to turn your vision into a reality. If you attach compelling reasons to your vision, you will naturally want to move on to the next steps. For example, Tom knows that before he can complete any other goal, he must prepare a Financial Independence Assessment. Once this is complete, he can begin detailing his family legacy goals.

SUPPORTING RESOURCES

The next step in the process is to inventory the strengths that you possess—financial, emotional, intellectual, and spiritual—along with key relationships. These resources all play a part in achieving your goals.

As an example, let's take a look at Tom's resources:

- His business is doing well.

- He and Paula have a strong asset base.

- Paula has a retirement income of $40,000 per year starting in five years.

- Tom and Paula agree that Tom needs to provide different control structures for the different children (and grandchild).

- Tom has no debt.

- Tom is disciplined.

- Tom and Paula share philanthropic goals.

Think of your resources as all the things that will work in your favor. Once you identify all of the supporting resources at your fingertips, you'll begin to see that you already have some of the power needed to achieve your vision and accomplish your goals. For instance, Tom has a supportive wife who understands that he must create different plans for each child. Paula's support will work in his favor as he begins making a plan to divide his assets. Knowing what you already have to meet your objectives will help you identify what resources you should add to your tool kit, and what resources you can lean on for support.

Before spending time putting together an action plan, it is important to identify whether there are enough supporting resources to implement goals. Planning is irrelevant if financial and other resources are not available. For instance, if Tom had a ton of debt and few assets, he would need to reprioritize his goals. Before considering a family legacy, for instance, he would need to figure out how to accumulate assets.

OBSTACLES

At times, obstacles will interrupt your progress toward success. Obstacles are life situations that are not part of your ideal vision. Until those situations are removed or handled, you will not be able to achieve your vision. Your vision cannot come to fruition with those obstacles still present.

Not all obstacles can be anticipated, but by identifying the likely ones, we can develop an "early warning system" to steer clear of them and not hit them head-on!

Here are some examples of obstacles:

- Credit card debt

- An estranged family

- Working at a job you do not enjoy

- Living in a part of the country you dislike

- Getting dismissed from work

- A sudden medical issue

- A family member's death or disability

These obstacles must be addressed, or they will inhibit your progress. All of these obstacles will stop you from moving toward your goals and truly achieving your vision.

Tom and Paula are beginning to think of Jennifer as a confidante as they reflect on the obstacles in their way. They rattle off a string of obstacles:

> "I have a blended family, and there are always a few hiccups when it comes to children from two marriages," says Tom.

> "All the senior business partners at my firm want to retire at about the same time. I suspect the water is going to be very muddy for a while," says Tom.

> "I have no idea whether my assets are sufficient to sustain my lifestyle and help me reach my family-legacy goals," says Paula.

> "We don't have an updated estate plan."

> "When it comes to gifting assets, we need to create different terms for all of the children and grandchild. In order to avoid conflict, we will have to clearly explain and clarify the reasoning behind each decision in order to be sensitive to each child's perception of what we are going to do."

> "I'm aging, and even though my health is good, it's not as great as it used to be," says Tom.

> "I'm not sure what will happen if Tom or I get sick," says Paula.

"My business doesn't have a succession plan. Really, it's kind of a mess. We don't know which path we will take—we would like to sell it to some of the junior partners, but we can't figure out how they can afford to buy it, so we might end up selling it to a competitor. Of course, we don't have any of the necessary documents, like a buy/sell agreement, nor have we developed strategies for lifetime buyouts or death buyouts," says Tom.

"We don't have life insurance."

"I feel a lot of pressure from people who want me to give them money. My university asked me for $500,000 to put my family name on a building. Paula's niece asked us to help her with startup funds. The problem is that I'm not sure she is experienced enough to start the business," says Tom.

Once you have listed all of the current obstacles, you can begin the process of approaching each obstacle in a strategic manner. One by one, you will begin to determine a strategy for overcoming each obstacle.

READY, SET, GO!

The last part of this process is to determine how ready you are to move forward with each of your goals. As you move forward, some goals will likely be abandoned, others may be put on the backburner, and others will be undertaken immediately. Even the decision to discard a goal you once thought important is progress, since the energy that would have been expended is then free to be redirected.

Readiness to implement those planning strategies that are important, that have supporting resources available, and whose obstacles have been eliminated is the final part of the VISOR model. We know that procrastination is one of the age-old challenges when it comes to planning. The

VISOR model identifies the need to take action: A great plan not implemented is no plan at all!

You must ask yourself: "How ready am I to do what is needed to overcome each obstacle?" If you are not ready at this point in time, that's okay. You will realize that you need to devise a timeline for attacking a particular obstacle. Each obstacle needs to be evaluated to determine your readiness to take action. You should prioritize your actions so that your resources are directed towards the most important obstacles first. Realizing that all of these obstacles that you have written down must be removed in order to realize your vision will galvanize you to begin the process of making your vision a reality.

As you prioritize the readiness to take action, make sure that, if certain actions have to be postponed, they aren't lost forever and dismissed. There is nothing wrong with not being able to tackle all goals or issues at once.

However, once you have a priority list of goals that need action, monitoring the action plan and having a timetable for the completion of long-term objectives are absolutely necessary.

Tom and Jennifer, for instance, know that they must tackle his Financial Independence Assessment and Family Legacy needs first and foremost. Only once these are complete will he be able to address other goals, such as business-succession planning.

When you look at the completed VISOR model, you will see a very clear picture of where you want to go. You will have an idea in your mind about what it is going to look like and feel like. You are going to identify why it is so important and why it makes you feel so good to have that vision as part of your life. You will have identified your supporting resources and what is stopping you from getting there. You will have isolated what obstacles need to be removed first, then second, and so on.

All that is left is to begin the journey toward making your vision a reality.

— KEY POINTS —

> If you can find the time and the right advisor who allows you to dream, you can create your own destiny.

> To bring a plan to fruition, you must follow a process. VISOR is a five-step process that allows you to uncover your dreams.

> 1. First, create your **V**ision and define your goals.
> 2. Next, prioritize your goals according to their **I**mportance.
> 3. Third, identify your **S**upporting resources.
> 4. Fourth, identify any real or potential **O**bstacles.
> 5. Finally, measure your **R**eadiness to take action.

> This process integrates the important elements that will provide the criteria by which you will monitor your family's wealth-optimization plan.

> You will greatly benefit from a VISOR review at least annually even if you already have a plan in place and believe all of your planning is done. This will reinforce that your plan is still relevant despite the changes that have occurred to you, your family, or within your business.

CHAPTER 4

Your Number: What Does It Mean?

Tom is worth $8.7 million. This includes:

- His interest in his business-consulting firm, worth $4 million.
- A $1.5 million retirement plan,
- Investments worth $1 million,
- Two homes worth $1.2 million, and
- An additional $1 million.

Young adults just getting started off in life might think this is a lot of money. Actually, given that the median household income in the United States in 2011 was about $50,000, this is a lot, even if you are nearing retirement age.

However, is this number enough to sustain Tom's lifestyle and accomplish his family legacy goals? Tom has no idea.

In *The Number*, Lee Eisenberg defines your Number simply: "How much money do you need to secure the rest of your life?" This might seem like a simple question, but Eisenberg had trouble finding anyone who could answer the question.

Can you answer the question? What is your Number?

If you cannot answer this question, you are not alone. To be sure, answering this question requires more than a simple formula, as you are about to learn.

YOUR NUMBER

Your Number provides a lot of insight into the stage you have reached in your financial life.

- **The Financial Dependence Stage:** If you are in this stage, you have not yet achieved financial independence. Until you have reached financial independence, you will likely be trying to close the gap between what you have and what you need. In other words, your Number becomes a target you are scrambling to reach. During this stage, protecting your resources is of secondary focus. Planning done at this stage tends to be more defensive in nature: wills, trusts, insurance, and the like.

- **The Financial Independence Stage:** If you are in this stage, you have reached financial independence. This stage is generally the most difficult to perceive. Many people erroneously believe they have reached financial independence, but when they begin searching to determine their Number, they realize they do not have enough money to sustain their lifestyle. On the other hand, other clients are shocked to learn that they achieved financial independence years ago. During this stage, protecting your financial resources might become the primary concern.

- **The Financial Transcendence Stage:** Individuals in this stage have achieved financial independence and focus on transferring resources to their heirs. Planning for this group is generally strategic. During this stage, clients begin to focus on how their financial assets can influence their social capital, human capital, and intellectual capital, as you will learn later.

The following diagram illustrates three life-planning stages. The diagram's purpose is to help you determine your stage of financial security. Although each stage has a particular planning focus, most of us need to plan in more than one stage at a time. There are three main categories, each with a primary and a secondary focus.

Stage	Life Stage	Primary Focus	Secondary Focus
Stage 1	Financial Dependence	Accumulate	Protect
Stage 2	Financial Independence	Protect	Accumulate/Transfer
Stage 3	Financial Transcendence	Transfer	Protect

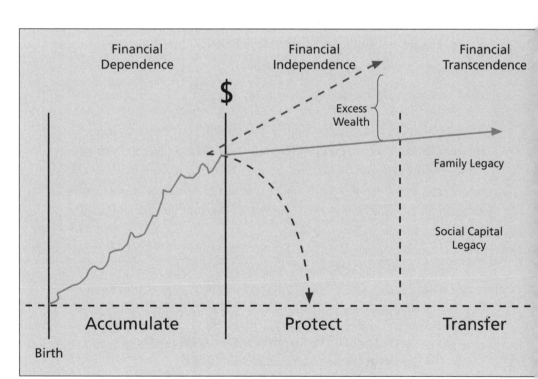

Regardless of which stage you are in, your Number is comprised of two definite categories:

1. First and foremost, the amount (or value) of assets you will consume (or use) to maintain the quality of life you want for you and your family.

2. The actual assets that you want to keep for your enjoyment—assets that will not produce income, but will be used by the family, such as boats, vacation homes, or recreational vehicles.

Your Number will also consist of specialized categories specific to your situation, such as:

✓ Start-up funds for future business opportunities.

✓ Investment funds that allow you to support other projects.

✓ Family funds that are earmarked to help children, grandchildren, or siblings meet goals.

✓ Emergency reserves.

Your Number might also include a "just in case" category that helps you feel confident and certain that your Number is sufficient. Over the years, you will review the categories that make up your Number, revising them so that you feel comfortable that your Number is realistic. As time and your confidence progresses, the "just in case" amount will become smaller and smaller.

As Tom, Paula, and Jennifer embark on his Financial Independence Assessment, they identify these categories, which will feed into their Number:

✓ The assets Tom and Paula need to maintain the quality of life they want for themselves and their family.

✓ The specific assets that Tom and Paula would like to maintain throughout their lifetime.

✓ Any special funds that Tom and Paula want to
supplement their lifestyle.

*How will we make money? Who will be the family's breadwinner? Do
we have enough money?* These are questions that everyone asks—from the
financially dependent to the financially transcendent. Everyone, including
the very affluent, is preoccupied with these worries. If you have a modest
salary and struggle to make your mortgage, you might think that once you
reach Financial Independence, these worries will be swept away. That said,
as the old adage goes, it's not how much you have, but how much you spend.
If you have not spent significant time considering your Number, you simply
will not know if you have enough.

In fact, this is the pebble in most people's shoe—harassing them
constantly as they try to take action. How can you take action if you do not
know where you are or what you need?

Knowing your Number will help you answer the following questions:

"What amount of wealth secures my family and me?"

"How much wealth do I need so that I will not outlive my
money?"

"How much saved money will it take to sustain the pur-
chasing power of my dollars throughout my life?"

"How much money needs to be set aside today to provide a
college education for my grandchildren?"

"How should I indentify average return to calculate the
growth of my investments (both pre- and post- retirement)?"

"How do I identify my risk tolerance?"

"How can I determine if I have discretionary capital to
help my children in their quest to achieve their dreams
without putting my lifestyle in jeopardy?"

> "How can I protect myself so that I will not run out of money too soon and thus have to move back in with my children?"
>
> "How can I support my community without affecting my family's desire for financial independence?"
>
> "How will I know I have accumulated all of my needed assets so that my Financial Independence is realized?"
>
> "How much extra capital will I need for protection against future taxes and inflation?"

Identifying your Number allows you to manage your financial choices regularly and develop contingencies. By creating your Number, you can choose to:

1. Close the gap between where you are now and where you need to be, if you are in the Financial Dependence Stage;

2. Feel confident that your resources are protected, if you are in the Financial Independence Stage; or

3. Begin or continue to use your financial assets to invest in your social, human, or intellectual capital, if you are in the Financial Transcendence Stage.

— WHAT YOUR NUMBER WILL DO FOR YOU —

Regardless of which stage you are in, you must know your Number to achieve it, maintain or increase it, and protect it. Knowing your Number helps you stay on track and act instead of react.

That said, your Number might change as you age, as your values shift, and as your financial circumstances evolve. When you are nineteen, your Number might be what it takes to get you through a long weekend! Yet as you mature, this number will take on a longer horizon and become an integral part of your life.

Many of our Wealth Coaches have had clients who could not answer what they required for financial independence. Once they looked at the actual numbers that they were spending in each of their categories, they were shocked. Did they need a yearly clothing budget of thousands of dollars? They could certainly afford it, but did they need it? They could afford a private plane, but was it really worth it? Did they really spend a third of their income per year on travel and entertainment? Did they care or was this a necessary part of their lifestyle that they really enjoyed? What were the trade-offs of having a high burn rate? Were they happier or more connected? For these families, discussing these issues was an education unto itself. They began discovering their truest values and then prioritizing the importance of these values.

Important to note is that each family is different, so there is no right or wrong answer to questions regarding how you spend your money. Your Number is unique to you, your mission, your vision, your value, and your goals.

To embrace your Number and continue to monitor it, you must have an exploratory process that gives you the space to consider both what you want and what is possible. After that, you need a methodology to help shape your vision and your Number as circumstances change. Without both pieces, you run the risk of an extended daydream session, where you wind up with nothing workable to begin formalizing your need.

This process should allow you to consider balancing various tradeoffs and outcomes; by doing so, you will be confident that you have considered every possibility. Your Number, whatever it turns out to be, must be one in which you and your family members can believe. Your Number will become your rudder against the winds of change; it is your commitment to a desired outcome.

This process is highly personal, and sometimes the most successful people have the most difficulty with it. These people are often high achievers—driven, intelligent, and hard-working. They have success and admiration by most public measures. However, the same personality that drives these people to achieve often prevents them from approaching the Number in the right way.

❖❖❖

Tom had always been on the go. He was young when he married Joyce (Evan and Laura's mother), and he worked 60-hour weeks, at a minimum. He was always working—even during vacations. Then he had Evan and Laura, and his priorities shifted; he worked 50-hour weeks, found ways to delegate, and brought on partners to help lessen the load.

When he wasn't at work, he was with the children, going to softball games, coordinating picnics, and hosting neighborhood barbeques.

Then he and Joyce divorced. He worried about college funds, worked a little more than he should have, and never had time to stop, breathe, and plan.

He married Paula, had another child, sent his older children to college, and ...

... life just kept going. Tom—a go-getter—never wanted to stop.

Now, at age 60, it seems absurd to him that he doesn't have a family wealth-optimization plan, much less know his Number. As he thinks about it, he realizes he has no idea how much he needs for financial independence. Is he already there? $8.7 million sure sounds like a lot, but given all his goals, is it?

Jennifer nods as Tom shares all this with her.

"If it makes you feel any better, a lot of people are in your same boat," Jennifer tells him. "In fact, successful people are often the ones who have the most planning to do. They spend all their time working hard and prioritizing, but somehow, those lower-priority tasks that deal with really important issues never make it to the top of the list. There's almost always something that seems more pressing than financial planning issues.

"These clients don't have a second to spare. As they accumulate assets, they don't have time to plan."

Jennifer suggests a strategy to help Tom and Paula determine their Number.

1. Establish a spending plan and determine how much they really need to provide for all their needs on an annual basis. This can be calculated on a weekly or monthly basis with the goal of reaching one number that identifies how much Tom, Paula, and their family spend annually. Jennifer explains that this number should not include:

- Personal savings.

- Contributions to any retirement plan.

- Any one-time or temporary expenditures, such as weddings, home remodelling, or special vacations.

- Any money that is being used to pay off debt that will not be present during retirement.

- Mortgage costs, if the mortgage will be paid before retirement.

- College savings, if this will be complete before retirement.

2. After Tom, Paula, and Jennifer determine the final amount that they spend annually, Jennifer asks them to envision how and where they want to live during retirement. She explains that if this requires more money, they should add an additional expense to the current lifestyle number determined in Step One.

    Jennifer explains that the ideal retirement requires expenses similar to the expenses before retirement. Some financial advisors discount retirement expenses by 20 percent or even 30 percent, expecting their clients to spend less money in retirement. Jennifer explains that she has not seen many wealthy clients who want to reduce their lifestyle simply because they have retired. In fact, for the first ten years after retirement, many people travel and take on hobbies and other activities they did not have time for during their working years.

    Jennifer adds another important point: "We are living longer and are healthier during retirement than our ancestors," she tells Tom and Paula. "So we don't automatically reduce our needs in retirement. They just shift to a different focus."

3. Jennifer explains that she also needs to know how long Tom and Paula expect to live (based on lifestyle and his parents' age at death).

    Jennifer gives them an excellent tip in determining their likely age at death: "Consider the life span of your parents and grandparents as a beginning point. Add ten years to adjust for the benefits of modern medicine."

4. The next step is to list the amount of money Tom and Paula will need each year to pay for their expenses, adding 3 percent to each subsequent year to adjust for inflation. If Tom determines in Step Three that he will live another 25 years, Tom will have 25 different annual expense numbers, each 3 percent more than the last.

5. Finally, Jennifer helps Tom and Paula add each of these yearly numbers together to determine the total retirement capital needed.

Next, Jennifer asks Tom to consider how much money he and Paula will be worth at retirement.

1. The process starts by determining when Tom and Paula want to retire.

2. Then, Tom and Paula consider what their retirement plan, personal savings, and additional income will be at retirement.

3. Jennifer explains that Tom and Paula should also add a rate of return on their saved money each year depending on how they intended to invest during retirement. "You might have a more aggressive rate in the first ten years and a more moderate rate for the remaining years of retirement," Jennifer says.

"Now that we know what your assets will be at retirement, we can compare this to your lifestyle needs to see if you are on track for your retirement needs," says Jennifer.

"Great," says Tom. "Once I know this, we can tackle our second goal of creating a family legacy."

"Exactly," says Jennifer. "It's impossible to plan your family legacy and social-capital legacy goals if you two are worried about taking care of your lifestyle needs!"

As part of Tom and Paula's family legacy, they:

1. Prepare a Survivor Income Assessment to clarify the capital required to provide for Paula (for the remainder of her life) and Kelly and Jackson (through their college education).

2. Establish goals for family-legacy objectives for Evan, Laura, Kelly, and Jackson. When determining the appropriate time to deliver inheritances, they evaluate three factors: 1) financial resources, based on their Number; 2) the various structures available for bequeathing money and assets; and 3) the different ages of the children and grandchildren. In the end, they establish different funding mechanisms for each child and grandchild.

3. Determine the availability of capital to support community programs. Together with Paula, Tom prepares a Social Capital Legacy Assessment, which determines how much money they can donate, as well as when the money will be donated, and the type of transfer that will be most appropriate.

4. Discuss the different strategies necessary to create the family legacy, such as:

   a. Modifying their current estate plans to consider the appropriate adjustments to their wills and trust mechanisms.

   b. Establishing a lifetime charitable remainder trust, which could be funded with the sale of Tom's business.

   c. Creating testamentary charitable remainder trusts for Paula, Kelly, and the community.

   d. Creating a family foundation as the recipient of remainder interest from the charitable remainder trust.

   e. Establishing a lifetime or testamentary charitable lead trust with the children and/or grandchildren (outright or in trust) as remainder beneficiaries.

— HOW DO WE DETERMINE YOUR NUMBER? —

Our approach to finding your Number addresses the three realms of financial planning: financial independence, family legacy, and social-capital legacy (such as charitable contributions). All three realms are considered when determining your Number, but this chapter focuses primarily on financial independence. Most clients are unable to focus on family-legacy or social-capital intentions until they are certain that they are financially secure. As such, this chapter places most of the emphasis on the task of determining whether your assets are sufficient enough to cover your lifestyle. In Chapters 5 and 6, we will address the important components of family-legacy and social-capital legacy, respectively. Once you are sure that you are financially independent, you can read these chapters, revisit your Number, and make changes that incorporate your social-capital and family-legacy intentions.

The initial steps of finding financial independence are common to all financial-planning exercises. Advisors take inventory of your assets, liabilities, income, and expenses. Assumptions are made about variables such as investment returns, the cost of living, and discounting rates. They then consider factors such as age and expected life span (or in other words, how long income is required). Some will also factor in legacy intentions (see Chapter 6) and philanthropic obligations.

For a young couple with minor savings, the prospect of accumulating $10 million to fund a retirement 40 years in the future can be intimidating. However, when the total value of the next 40 years of accumulated income is brought into the picture, the perception of the gap changes and the seemingly unrealistic amount is narrowed considerably.

Our model looks at the resources you have available for financial independence:

1. Your financial capital (your assets); and
2. Your capital potential (your income for the rest of your working years).

These values are then compared to your financial-independence goal. The model allows you to delete selected assets from the equation, which you can plan to leave to your children or to your favorite charity. As your working years dwindle, your capital-potential resources will diminish. Your hope is that your assets have increased at a better than or equal pace.

In your younger years, the critical planning has to do with protecting and insuring your employment earnings. This number may be 90 percent of your financial-independence resources! Closer to your retirement, when assets have accumulated, the biggest focus is on attention to your rate of return, as well as inflation.

Being 100-percent financially independent does not necessarily mean that you can rely on existing assets to fund your lifestyle. As previously discussed, a younger couple may be relying to a large extent on their future income stream. At this stage, it is important that this future income stream be protected and secured in the event of death or disability. As time goes by and income is converted into assets, securing the return on the asset becomes more important. The unique result of this process is that financial independence can be measured as a percentage. If you have less than 100 percent of your Number, you must plan to increase income or return on assets. If you have more than 100 percent, you can use your excess resources for other purposes.

Most of our work is with people who are more than 100-percent financially independent. We have found that a common theme exists with many of these people, in particular with those who are first-generation clients. They started with nothing, and they often have an underlying fear that everything could be lost. Because of this, their wealth remains locked up—just in case! Their focus continues to be on frugality, saving, and accumulating. Though philanthropy, helping out relatives and rewarding key employees are important to these clients, the time never seems quite right. As a result, they feel a void when it comes to their social-capital legacy.

At the heart of this issue is the lack of clarity around the Number. Those families who are clear on their Number will structure their affairs so that this number can never be compromised. After that, they are free to unlock their excess wealth for family-legacy and social-capital-legacy planning. With clear consciences, they are able to direct their excess wealth by:

1. Escalating their lifestyle,
2. Assisting family and friends financially,
3. Investing in business opportunities, and/or
4. Directing more to philanthropy.

If you have less than 100 percent of your Number, you have three choices: You must plan to increase income, increase the rate of return on your assets, or reduce your expenditure goals.

One way or another, the clear understanding and knowledge that you have found your Number, or financial independence, can bring liberation and exuberance. This benefits not only you, but also generations of your family to come. The community in which you live can also benefit from your generosity.

— KEY POINTS —

> In its simplest form, your Number represents the amount of money you need to secure the rest of your life. Your Number is determined by: 1) considering different categories of your life and assigning a dollar value to each of these categories; and 2) considering your net worth and retirement goals, and comparing this to the amount of money you will spend over the course of your life to maintain your lifestyle.

> Even people with a tremendous amount of wealth often do not know their Number. Many people surpass their own financial expectations but increase their spending along the way. This prevents them from reaching their goals earlier. Rarely do they have a target number in mind throughout their wealth creation. Oftentimes, these people are surprised at the actual value of their total holdings. Having never seen their net worth in its entirety, they are surprised to see the value of the family business, real estate, life insurance, retirement savings, and the like. Had these people been more aware of their Number, they might have reined in spending that did not support their goals, which would have allowed them to realize their goals at a much earlier age.

> Knowing your Number allows you to manage your financial choices based on a concrete Number and your values.

> Your Number is based on the three realms of financial planning: financial independence, family legacy, and social-capital legacy. All three realms are considered when determining your Number, but this chapter focused primarily on financial independence. Most clients are unable to focus on social-capital and family legacy until they are certain that they are financially secure.

> Learning your Number allows you to close the gap between where you are and where you need to be. On the other hand, clients who have more available capital than their Number can begin focusing on the family-legacy and social-capital legacy components of their planning.

CHAPTER 5

Wealth: Is It All About the Money?[5]

Tom is worth $8.7 million. His business interest is worth $4 million; his homes, investments, and holdings are worth $3.2 million, and his retirement plan is worth $1.5 million. On paper, anyone can tell that Tom is wealthy.

However, a financial statement barely gives the full picture. Tom's advisors can tell a lot about Tom's assets and income by looking at a piece of paper, but this information is not as important as learning about the things by which he is emotionally motivated. In fact, the details of Tom's assets and income might be the least important of all the information his advisors know about him. During Jennifer's first conversation with Tom, she learned that family is Tom's most important value. He has a passion for helping people learn. He is generous and compassionate. He surprises people with his mischievous sense of humor. He loves to travel. He spends his weekends hiking and teaching Jackson and Kelly how to fish. He could listen to his older children debate politics and never get bored.

These values are not reflected in Tom's financial statement. Yet, he has communicated that they are more important to him than anything he owns.

What's the first thing that comes to your mind when you hear the word *wealth*? Do you picture fat stacks of greenbacks? How about a suitcase full

---

5 The authors are indebted to James ("Jay") E. Hughes, Jr., for his philosophy of wealth as expounded in his book, *Family Wealth: Keeping It in the Family*. This chapter, this book, and our work are grounded in Jay's philosophy.

of cash bundles? Most people associate wealth with financial assets. When considering whether a person is successful, most of us take into account his or her bank account or real-estate holdings.

Let us paint a different picture of wealth. Consider, instead, your value as a wealth-holder and also your values as a human being. This definition certainly considers your monetary worth, but it also takes into account the vital impact that you have on family members, friends, your work associates, and your community. These factors do not involve money or property at all, but if you have a positive impact on the people about whom you care, you are certainly a wealth-holder.

Just think of Ebenezer Scrooge from *A Christmas Carol*. Miserly Scrooge had stacks of gold coins but no one with whom to spend the holidays. On the other hand, his trusted and underpaid clerk, Bob Cratchit, had a wonderful family and many dear friends. Who was the truly wealthy man in the scenario?[6]

As you hear the word *wealth*, think about the people who mean the most to you. Close your eyes and picture their faces. See their smiles and the color of their eyes. Hear their infectious laughter. Is this a better definition of wealth in your life?

As we talk about wealth, remember that our definition considers wealth to be more than money! To truly help a person become wealthy or maintain wealth, an advisor must focus not only on financial capital, but also on human, social, and intellectual capital.

Yet most current models of financial planning focus on financial wealth only. Many clients and advisors think of wealth as the difference between what one owns and what one owes, often referred to as "capital," which is usually measured in dollars. As a result, a direct correlation is made to capital as a sign of success, and wealth is considered the final ingredient to calculate the amount of success achieved.

When value is left out of the equation, a huge portion of a person's wealth is overlooked. Too many advisors begin wealth discussions by asking for a list of financial assets. Any list of the tangible, easily measured

---

6 The Masai people of Africa believe that leaving many children is a sign of wealth. As a nomadic people, the Masai do not consider money to have much value (if any at all), but leaving children to continue the existence of the tribe is highly valuable.

belongings that you own leads to discussions about each asset, about what you want to do with each asset, and what will happen to the asset after it has been used or distributed.

This approach restricts the subject matter too much, which in turn restricts the scope of the discussion. The conversation is reduced to an overview of "quantitative data." Intangible assets are excluded, because they cannot be easily measured. However, we do emphasize the importance of determining how sentimental items of little monetary value but tremendous sentimental value are passed to heirs and the next generation.

Can you really begin to have a discussion about wealth if it ignores a significant part of what you value in your life?

Abraham Maslow, an American psychologist, formulated "Maslow's Hierarchy of Needs," a theory of developmental psychology. Maslow believed that once our most basic needs for food, clothing, and shelter are met, we seek to satisfy other important needs. The higher we climb up the hierarchy, the more sophisticated our needs become, eventually seeking recognition and self-actualization.

Most of you living in North America have met your most basic needs. Yet it is highly unlikely that any financial planner has helped you climb up the hierarchy by asking this simple question: *What makes you happy?*

Instead, you and your advisors most likely continue to create strategies so that you can collect more and more financial capital. As you climb up the hierarchy, this measure of wealth becomes less important. Rather than collecting more money, you now need to measure your wealth in relation to the people and activities that make you happy.

— THE FOUR KINDS OF WEALTH —

Think beyond the dollar signs and the cha-ching of the cash register to consider non-assets you can possess but not own: safety, security, freedom, friendships, and the like.

The common thread for all of these abstractions, feelings, and needs is that when we identify them as wealth, they immediately become valuable. Wealth coaches understand that what is valuable to one person may or may not be valuable to another. Although we can all agree on the objective value (also known as "societal recognition") of dollars, cars, and buildings, everyone will assign a different subjective value to the intangibles such as safety, security, and the freedom to do what he or she wants.

Measuring capital in more than just dollars is important. With this comes a realization that a family's assets are its members. In this way, a family's wealth consists of its members' human, intellectual, and social capital.

When considering values and valuables, wealth consists of four forms of capital structures:

✓ **Human Capital:** Who are you, and who are the members of your family? What are each family member's talents and capabilities, and how have these contributed to other family members?

✓ **Intellectual Capital:** This is your family's collective knowledge. While individuals know a lot of information, pooling that knowledge can create a magnifying effect benefiting all family members.

✓ **Social Capital:** Beyond charitable contributions, social capital covers how your family interacts with the larger community (civic engagement), as well as family members' social networks and extension of caring for those outside the family.

✓ **Financial Capital:** This is the best-known of all forms of capital. Measured by assets, financial capital is the raw material that supports the three other capitals.

Let's consider these forms of capital one at a time.

HUMAN CAPITAL

The human capital of a family consists of the individuals who make up the family. A family might include immediate family, extended family, or close friends and their offspring.[7] Thus, when assessing human capital,

---

7 Though the example used throughout this book focuses on a husband-wife-blended-family structure, there is no "typical" family. Your family might include children; it might include siblings, nieces, and nephews. You might have no "blood" family, instead considering your close friends (and perhaps their children) to be your family. Regardless, the strategies in this book apply to you and your family, however defined.

a family must consider how it addresses the physical and emotional well-being of each family member. How is the family investing in each member to assist that individual in achieving his or her maximum well-being? Why is achieving such a state of well-being important? A family, like an investor, must look to maximize its return on capital if the family (and each of its members) is to achieve the growth (personal and financial) necessary to impact future generations and the communities in which they will live.

> DANCER MARTHA GRAHAM once said, "There is a vitality, a life force, an energy, a quickening that is translated through you into action, and because there is only one of you in all of time, this expression is unique. And if you block it, it will never exist through any other medium and it will be lost. The world will not have it."
>
> Indeed, work is critical to a person's self-worth, particularly if the work is an expression of that person's unique ability.

To maximize human capital:

1. Each member of the family must be viewed as a unique asset capable of providing something inimitable to the family and community. Accordingly, the family leadership must gain insight and help develop each member's unique ability by learning about each member's passions. Once identified, family leadership must determine how to apply financial capital to each member's unique ability. This might include:

   - Education.

   - Mentoring (within or outside the family).

   - Learning experiences and internships.

   - Financial "hand-ups" when the going gets tough. ("Hand-ups" are different than "hand-outs" in that the former is given only to qualifying family members who can use the financial capital to make a contribution. This contribution might be made to humanity, such as a piece of music; it might be to a missionary cause, in the form of helping starving children, for instance; or it might be to a business in the form of creating a return for investors.)

2. Specific family values must be established, and family members must have ongoing dialog about how these values are practiced.

3. The family unit must be concerned for each member's physical and spiritual well-being, including physical health and mental health. This calls for encouragement of healthy lifestyles and activities that promote mental health.

4. The family unit should emphasize the importance of each individual's self-worth, well-being, and pursuit of happiness.

5. To promote human capital, the family should be purposeful about spending time together (as a group and one-on-one) to develop a love and appreciation for one another that lead to a desire on the part of all members to be known as a "family."

INTELLECTUAL CAPITAL

Intellectual capital can best be summarized as such: Life has presented each of you with a broad or specialized knowledge base! Each family member's academic success, artistic success, and interpersonal successes add to the family's collective knowledge. In fact, you might be surprised at how useful all this collective knowledge can be. Intellectual capital might be as mundane as where to buy the freshest produce; it might be scholarly, such as expertise in Civil War history. It might be an artistic talent, or it might be a life-saving connection: Your maternal first cousin has a paternal first cousin who is the best brain surgeon in the country and can get you that crucial appointment tomorrow.

People who fail to understand the degree and depth of intellectual capital possessed by their family members are at a great risk of losing this intellectual capital. Those who take steps to understand, value, and preserve their extended intellectual capital can perpetuate a legacy for generations to come.

If each family member's intellectual capital is to be harnessed for the greater good of the family, the following issues might be explored:

1. How wide of a net will you cast over the term "family" in an effort to have your family members share their talents, knowledge, and insight with other members? Will you include grandparents, parents, siblings, children, nieces and nephews, cousins, grandchildren, and close family friends?

2. How do you nurture, collect, categorize, and disseminate the accumulated knowledge of all family members?

3. Will you develop a written collection of family stories that share some of the accumulated knowledge and wisdom of past and current family members in order to permanently record them for sharing through the generations?

4. How do you encourage family members to stretch themselves intellectually and continue adding to the collective intellectual capacity of the family?

5. Do you emotionally and financially encourage family members to study other cultures so that the family can gain intellectual insight into an ever-shrinking world?

SOCIAL CAPITAL

John Donne had it right when he wrote, "No man is an island." Likewise, no family exists separate and apart from its community. You interact with those around you either purposefully or by daily happenstance. Social capital considers how you interact and relate to the world in two sets of circumstances: (1) when interacting with others, and (2) when interacting with your community.

As you think about your personal relationships, consider that some people have greater impact on your life than others. Who surrounds you can have significant impact because their relationship has influence on the activities of your life. Think about the three to five people outside of your family with whom you have the most contact. Who are they? What are they about? What do they value? How do they see themselves and their place in the world? Are they a reflection of what you value? If not, are the relationships providing you something that makes them worthwhile, even if the relationships cause conflict? How do the relationships influence the growth and development of your family's human and intellectual capital? Are the relationships enriching, and what do they say about your family?

Families with large amounts of social capital have invested time to establish a network of personal and professional relationships. Often the quantity and quality of "knob turners" will define the family's ability to accomplish some of the important family social goals. Often referred to as "networking," this activity should not be considered akin to social-ladder climbing, whereby knob turners say all the "right" things so they can get into the "right" groups and self-promote the family. Rather, networking is about pursuing relationships with people who can add to a family's intellectual capital, emotionally support the family's human capital, and strengthen the family's values. Networking can also occur with individuals outside the family structure who have wealth and want to make a difference.

Your interactions with your community often are born out of your personal commitment and sense of respect, compassion, and concern for others. In this way, social capital is often expressed by assisting within communities by providing resources (time, talent, or treasures) to groups and organizations that align with your family or individual values. Commitment is usually expressed in one of two general ways:

1. Service in the form of giving your time and talent to any organization or directly to an individual or family in need of assistance.

2. Philanthropy in the form of your family's financial capital, which is used to build resources on behalf of an organization, or to fund activities and services in furtherance of your family's values.

Properly structured financial capital used to further philanthropic goals may provide income-tax and estate-tax reductions. A full discussion of the rules regarding charitable giving is beyond the scope of this book. A family or individual who wants to commit to a number of different projects can often leverage assets and extend the overall impact of the available resources. Those who want to create a significant lifetime or post-death continuing financial commitment to philanthropy, while also creating a significant family legacy, have many options available. One objective is not accomplished at the expense of the other.

FINANCIAL CAPITAL

Financial capital is a list of your material assets, such as stocks, bonds, investments, real estate and commodities, businesses, and other valuables. Financial assets feed and are fed by your family's human, intellectual, and social capital. Only after you develop and understand the first three capital structures can you assign financial assets to your family's goals, needs, and priorities of human, intellectual, and social capital.

Let us explain further. Without people (human capital), intelligence (intellectual capital), and society (social capital), financial capital would be impossible. Once financial capital is created, it can be used to strengthen people, intelligence, and society.

HUMAN + INTELLECTUAL + SOCIAL = FINANCIAL

Financial capital is seed money that you use to promote and grow all the other capitals you possess. Imagine, however, if you had no human, intellectual, or social capital. What good would your financial resources be to you then, Ebenezer Scrooge? They wouldn't be worth a farthing!

Your financial capital is the only kind of wealth that can be expressed with a fixed, quantitative number. The other kinds of wealth are qualitative, and they will vary among different people and different family groups.

❖❖❖

Your new definition of wealth considers that wealth is in the eyes of the beholder. In other words, wealth for each of you is what each of you perceives as valuable within the realm of human, social, and intellectual capital.

As noted previously, value can be set in terms of the tangible—land, cars, cash, or clothes. The land has an agreed-upon market value; the bank accounts have a finite number of dollars. However, what is the market price of a good marriage or a trusted relationship with a brother? What would you pay for a belief system that helps you succeed, day after day? You can own and measure a tangible asset. You cannot own the intangible, but you can nonetheless measure or assign a value to it.

Once you recognize that what is valued may be different for each of you, you should be able to agree that wealth has a unique meaning to each person. It should be obvious that using, improving, enhancing, and preserving your wealth become a different life's journey for each family member.

Within family wealth structures, the human, social, and intellectual elements give you the "why" and "for whom" of the financial assets. When you understand the personal dimension of your value definition, you can begin to develop a clearer picture of your intentions for the use of your financial assets.

If you have a clear understanding of how much money you will need to support your chosen lifestyle (see Chapter 4: Your Number), you can make plans regarding your excess wealth.

How might you allocate that capital to put it to its best use? You might ask yourself how the money can be used. You might consider reframing your definition of wealth from your bank account balances to your most valuable relationships. How can your financial wealth best carry out your mission, vision, values, and goals as they relate to your most important relationships? Are there ways your financial wealth can support your family, community, religion, and philanthropy?

You do not operate in a financial desert. Your financial planning will have an effect on your other three capitals, like it or not.

❖❖❖

When considering the Family Legacy and the financial capacity of Tom's children, Tom and Paula pay close attention to Tom's oldest daughter. Laura works for a nonprofit organization. She is passionate about her job, and she has job security. However, she must live frugally, and she will probably never receive much in the form of a raise.

However, she is responsible, intelligent, and capable. Because Tom is interested in strengthening his family unit, he and Paula consider how to help Laura find financial security while still treating Evan, who earns six figures, fairly and with respect.

Eventually, they decide that Tom will present this strategy to his two adult children:

For every two dollars gifted to Laura, Tom and Paula will put one dollar into a fund that Tom, Paula, and Jackson (Evan's son) will use to fund a charity of their choice. This strategy:

- Allows Tom and Paula to provide Laura with stronger financial security.

- Creates an opportunity for Tom and his grandson to strengthen their bond while choosing charitable activities.

- Helps Paula bond with Jackson and, through Jackson, with Evan.

- Shows both adult children that Tom respects and cares for them as unique individuals.

When considering how your financial capital can strengthen your family's human, social, and intellectual capital, remember that the soundest decisions support your values and contribute to building or preserving your human, intellectual, or social capital. You might consider assisting with your child's school's building fund instead of paying for excellent seats at your alma mater's football games. This decision has a direct relationship to your child's intellectual capital. You might not approve of the building program and instead decide to give to a football team as a way of strengthening your social capital. Neither decision is incorrect, so long as it is informed!

Installing a diverse system to monitor and measure your four capitals can take time and money; certainly it is not for everyone. Think about it for a minute before you give up on that idea. When you make your New Year's resolutions, are you not engaging in a similar process?

Listing goals and aspirations and then looking at them from time to time as you make decisions throughout the year are not too burdensome. Thinking about them now will change your outlook and intentionality about your four choices of capitals.

When you think about everything that is important to you, make sure that your legacy plan covers those areas of special concern. Your plan must address the values that are most important to you. Your current plan may be falling short of your objectives.

Take the challenge and consider whether or not your existing plan was developed from a traditional approach that addressed only the monetary aspect of your wealth. Think about a new approach that allows you to plan for the perpetual transfer of your non-monetary assets to the people you care about most.

TOUCHING BASE

THINK BACK to the five most important events that have occurred in your life. Perhaps it was the birth of your child, your wedding day, or the day you started your business. Relive them. Imagine them. Feel them. Try to experience them anew.

Now you are ready to answer this question: How many of these situations involved money?

If the answer to the question is "more than one," we would be really surprised! Most likely, none of them involved money!

Wealth: It's more than money!

— KEY POINTS —

> The definition of wealth should be expanded to include:

- **Human Capital:** Who are you, and who are the members of your family? What are each family member's talents and capabilities, and how are these contributed to other family members?

- **Intellectual Capital:** This is your family's collective knowledge. While individuals know a lot of information, pooling that knowledge can cause a magnifying effect, benefiting all family members.

- **Social Capital:** Beyond charitable contributions, social capital covers how your family interacts with the larger community (civic engagement), as well as family members' social networks and extension of caring for those outside the family.

- **Financial Capital:** This is the best-known of all forms of capital. Measured by assets, financial capital is the raw material that supports the three other capitals.

> Our new definition of money considers that wealth is not what it appears to be. In addition to tangible financial assets, wealth includes the intangible valuables within the realm of human, social, and intellectual capital.

CHAPTER 6

Your Footprints... Your Legacy

"**Imagine your grandchildren** and great-grandchildren during a holiday. Will the family be all together?"

Tom and Paula are in another estate-planning session, and Jennifer is asking tough questions again. In fact, she has given Tom and Paula one heck of an assignment: They are supposed to consider the legacy they want to pass down to their children, grandchildren, and great-grandchildren by answering the following questions:

- "Will your family members have a strong sense of where they came from?"

- "Will they know about the values, story, and events that shaped your family?"

- "Will the family traditions of the future resemble the special things you do today?"

- "If the topic of conversation turns to memories of holidays past, what might be said about those earlier gatherings?"

- "What might be said about you? How will they remember the atmosphere of your home and the mood of the gatherings celebrated there?"

- "Will your great-grandchildren even know your name?"

This last question shakes Tom's core. Though he is sure his parents and grandparents had talked about his great-grandparents, he cannot remember any of their first and last names. It breaks Tom's heart to imagine that Jackson's children might not know his name!

Can **you** remember your great-grandparents' first and last names on both sides of your family? If you cannot, you are not alone. In just three generations, we seem to lose connection with our ancestors. The names you do remember are typically because of someone's unique story.

Intentionally planning your legacy not only ensures that you are remembered, but it also dictates how you will be remembered. What kind of stories do you hope future generations will tell about you? What is going to be your legacy?

Let's start with this question: What is a legacy?

Legacy is often defined as how you will be remembered when you are gone. Although this is an important component of a legacy, it is far too limiting to capture the whole picture. Though this is the first component of legacy planning, we add a second component as well.

Legacy consists of two components:

1. How you will be remembered when you are gone.

2. Whom you will impact while you are alive.

Component #1
How will you be remembered when you are gone?

At some point in time in our lives, we all come to ask ourselves: *How will I be remembered after I am gone? What footprints will I leave?* The sad truth is that you probably will not be remembered unless you achieve celebrity status. If you are not a famous politician, actor, musician, or notorious criminal, your great-grandchildren will likely not remember your name ...

Unless you make a specific plan to leave a legacy.

This is why the second component of legacy is so important. If you want to leave a legacy, you must focus on whom you will impact—and how you will go about making this impact—while you are living.

Component #2
<u>Whom do you want to impact while you are living, and how?</u>

Let's imagine a legacy consisting only of the first component, without this crucial second component. You might establish trusts for your grand-children to fund their college educations. They would appreciate this, but would this impact their character? Even if they knew your name, they probably would not know much about your values or personality.

Wouldn't you be better able to pass along your values if you coupled financial resources with actions that your family members and loved ones witness while you are alive? This can be as simple as establishing traditions that your family members pass on to future generations, or they can be more complex, such as establishing trusts with the intention of passing along certain values.

— IT'S MORE THAN MONEY —

Many people feel that leaving a legacy is something only the ultra-rich do. These people mistakenly believe that they can leave a legacy only by naming a hospital wing or a building at their alma mater.

A legacy is not defined by money. Though the real property, trust mechanisms, and money you leave behind are the first components of a legacy, the memory you leave behind as a result of the second component is perhaps the more important part of your legacy.

In fact, your legacy is not defined by how wealthy you are. Do you think a poor person must leave any less of a legacy than a wealthy person? The accomplishments of Mother Teresa certainly prove that a person without any financial resources can leave a giant impact on the world.

Donating money is not the "Holy Grail" of creating a legacy. Phil-anthropic gifts can be highly rewarding and can make a huge impact on improving the quality of life for many, but that result alone does not define an individual's legacy. A legacy consists of the ripples you create in the water—ripples that crest into magnificent waves.

❖❖❖

Ever since Kelly was born 13 years ago, Tom has insisted on having dinner once a week with his entire family. After meeting with Jennifer, Tom decides that family dinner will also include a family meeting. Everyone will be encouraged to talk about his or her week's victories, opportunities, and obstacles. Each family member will also be asked to share one idea that will bring the family closer.

At first, Evan and Laura are skeptical, but Kelly and Jackson are enthusiastic. Jackson wants the family to have a talent show after family dinner. Kelly wants to create a family scrapbook with a page devoted to each member of her immediate family, as well as her grandparents, aunts and uncles, great-grandparents, and cousins.

"I could even make a page for Uncle Louie," says Kelly. Uncle Louie is actually Kelly's great, great, great uncle, an artist who became famous posthumously. Tom's hometown is filled with murals and architectural embellishments created by Uncle Louie.

Tom quietly reflects on Kelly's awareness of Uncle Louie. She probably has little knowledge of her ancestors, but she remembers Uncle Louie's name because he accomplished something unique.

"Kelly, that's a fantastic idea," says Tom. "Does anyone else have any ideas?"

Kelly and Jackson's enthusiasm is contagious, and eventually, Laura and Evan jump on board.

"I've been thinking about Jackson's birthday," says Evan. "I am always really thankful for how generous everyone is during birthdays and Christmas. However, I keep hearing stories about parents who have a nightmare-of-a-time keeping up with their children's standards. I am afraid Jackson is going to start to expect a lot of presents—and that just isn't what Christmas and birthdays are about."

Evan continues, "What if we all agreed to give each other just one present during birthdays and Christmas? Instead of shopping until we drop, we can all come up with a way to create a special memory with each member of our family. For instance, Kelly could create a photo collage or write a letter about her favorite memories of the year that would have impact. Paula, I'd be honored if you would give me a few cooking lessons. How do you make this fabulous beef bourguignon?"

Paula is beaming. Spending some quality time with Evan would be better than any material gift he could give her.

Laura pipes in: "What if we created Fun Funds?" she asked. "Those of us who want to give a financial gift can put it in a designated Fun Fund."

"What do you mean?" asks Kelly.

"We could create a savings account so that we have money to do something fun," says Laura. "For instance, for your birthday and Christmas, I will contribute money to the Laura and Kelly Fun Fund. We can pick something fun we want to do, and then we can use the Fun Fund to go and do it."

"Will you take me hiking?" says Kelly.

Laura has just returned from a week-long hiking trip to the Wind River Mountains in Wyoming. Her adventure was complete with bears in the campground, altitude sickness, and hailstorms.

"You must be crazy," Paula says to Kelly, laughing.

Tom concurs, and the thought of Kelly and Laura facing bears and hailstorms makes his stomach drop. Still, he can't help but sit back and smile. He can think of nothing better than watching Laura and Kelly plan for a big adventure.

"Great idea," Tom finally tells Laura. "I'm on board with having Fun Funds instead of gifts, especially if it means that I won't get another reindeer sweater from Paula."

Paula gives Tom a playful swat as the children all share a laugh.

Though we focus primarily on family members, true legacies impact all of our loved ones. This can include friends, clients, or those served by our non-profit organization.

Your legacy can come in three forms: your time, your talents, and your treasures. Anyone, regardless of socioeconomic status, has these three things.

- Your **time** has nothing to do with your net worth. Instead, it might be your commitment to volunteering for a specific cause or organization. It costs nothing to spend a few hours every week teaching your grandchild how to create a budget, set financial goals, and manage wealth. It costs nothing to teach him or her how to water-paint, fly-fish, volunteer, or play chess.

- **Talent** refers to a skill or expertise you have. You could create a legacy by coaching a sport (even when your family is not involved), or teaching a class in your local community.

- **Treasures** are most often specifically related to your ability to give financial contributions to specific causes, organizations, or research, but this does not have to be the case. Often, cash-poor people own family heirlooms that can leave a legacy. A scrapbook of old photos can tell the story of a great-grandfather who immigrated to the United States, set up shop as a iron worker, and created a solid foundation for his family.

A COMPLETE LEGACY addresses two things: the ways in which you will be remembered after you are gone, and what you are doing right now to make a difference to causes you care about and to the people you love. Your legacy is not something that will bear fruit only in the future. Your legacy can change lives today and can shape the world around you.

— HOW TO LEAVE A LEGACY —

Your will or revocable trust is the legal document that will ensure that the first part of your legacy is dealt with in the manner of your choosing. Unfortunately, many people do not have wills or revocable trusts, or if they do, the documents do not reflect their true wishes.

If you have a will or revocable trust, ask yourself this: *Does it allow you to transfer everything you have, to whom you want, when you want, and the way you want?* Do not forget that many assets, such as life-insurance benefits, annuities, retirement plans, employee-benefit plans, joint-tenancy property, and payable-on-death accounts, are passed along outside of your will or revocable trusts. Many of these assets have beneficiary designations that must be coordinated with your will or trust.

To get you started along the right track to leaving a meaningful legacy, you must invest time with your advisors in the Discovery Process. This process will help you answer key questions about your purpose in life, your mission, and what your values and goals are. Those answers will provide the foundation for a plan that accurately reflects what you want your legacy to be.

Though Tom and Paula have given generously to many charities over the years, their charitable giving feels a little bit empty, so they arrange a meeting with Jennifer to talk about their legacy plans.

Jennifer suggests that they also bring Tom's other advisors to the table.

"You will notice that all of the players on the team will have specific roles. Andrew will find financial products that will support your legacy goals. I'll design wills, trusts, foundations, or whatever other legal structures we need. Your accountant, business consultant, and planned-giving team members will also have jobs to do," Jennifer explains.

Jennifer also wants to use this opportunity to make sure that Tom and Paula's other advisors are fully on board with the values-based financial-planning model she is using (the Wealth Optimization System). She plans to review Tom and Paula's documented goals, as articulated in their VISOR worksheets from Chapter 3.

Leaving a legacy requires you to craft strategies to transfer your values to, or use your values to impact, those important people in your life. This is a highly personal journey that is best taken with the help of an advisor who specializes in mechanisms that allow your valuables to best impact your values and your human capital. You and your Wealth Coach might discuss such things as:

- Establishing "family meetings." Just as a business has meetings to discuss critical issues and next steps, families can and should meet to articulate what makes your family unique and what binds you together. Some Wealth Coaches might help you develop a "family mission statement" that describes your family's purpose.

- Drafting an ethical will that explains the moral fiber of your family.

- Your one-, three-, five-, and ten-year goals.

When Tom and Paula meet with their team of advisors, they walk away with several strategies designed specifically for them.

When Tom and Paula consider what is truly important to them, Paula realizes that she has a passion for helping single-parent families. Her passion stems from watching her mother struggle to support Paula and her three older siblings. Paula was born and raised in a destitute city in Central America. Her father died when she was two, and her mother was forced to raise the family alone. Tom, on the other hand, has a passion for learning. Together with their advisors, Tom and Paula decide to establish a foundation to help single mothers in Paula's country of birth receive an education. They intend not only to fund this venture but also to devote their time to its setup. Both of their lives have taken on a new purpose and passion; this will be one of their legacies.

Tom and Paula ask their advisors to establish a strategy that allows them to fund an existing foundation that provides scholarships to worthy students. Tom and Paula then make gifts to the foundation in Evan, Laura, and Kelly's names. The children then must work together to advise the foundation on how to allocate the scholarships.

Because Tom cannot stand the thought of being forgotten by the time Jackson's children are born, he and Paula ask Evan and Laura to videotape them talking about their lives, their parents, and the other important events that stand out in their minds. This is the action step Tom is most excited about, and it has nothing to do with his financial assets.

As they leave the meeting, Tom realizes that if he had never met Jennifer, he would have thought of legacy in terms of money only, and he would have overlooked other profound aspects of legacy-planning.

If you agree that non-financial assets such as your values, your life story, your work ethic, and your family culture are worth preserving, the next logical question is: How? A Wealth Coach can help you customize a plan.

— KEY POINTS —

> A complete legacy addresses two things:

1. The ways in which you will be remembered after you are gone; and

2. What you are doing right now to make a difference in the lives of the people you consider part of your human capital.

> Your legacy can come in three forms: your time, your talents, and your treasures.

1. **Time** has nothing to do with your net worth. Instead, it encompasses the time spent passing along your values or using your abilities to impact the world around you.

2. **Talent** refers to a skill and expertise you have and how you use these to create a lasting impression.

3. **Treasures** are those assets or material possessions that can be passed along.

> Leaving a legacy requires you to craft specific strategies that pass along your unique goals.

After learning about human, social, and intellectual capital, if you agree that non-financial assets—such as your values, your life story, your work ethic, and your family culture—are worth preserving, the next logical question is: How do I preserve them?

Our method is to use a planning approach with a central theme that emphasizes discovery of your mission, vision, values, and goals, such as the one described in this book.

> The authors, and other like-minded Wealth Coaches, can facilitate the discussions necessary to create a customized plan. Read on to learn that creating a plan is not enough. The plan you create must also have a process attached to it that sustains and updates the vision—as well as all the attendant strategies, tools, and tactics—that you articulate and capture.

CHAPTER 7

Building Your Team

Jennifer is telling Tom and Paula about her nephew's high school football game.

"He is the kicker," she says. "This means he's really got just one job—to kick that ball into the end zone."

Tom is listening, but he is a little confused as to why Jennifer is telling him about all of this. He already knows what a kicker does.

Then Jennifer clarifies.

"A football team is a great analogy for a client's planning needs," she says. "Accomplishing your goals is kind of like winning the Super Bowl. Before you even make the playoffs, you have to overcome some obstacles. By finding a team with the right strengths, and placing them in the appropriate positions, you can overcome these obstacles and reach your goals."

You have probably already engaged professionals to help you in some of the areas you would like to explore, but if you are like most clients, your team members are lacking a cohesive structure. Instead, these individual professionals are performing their duties in individual silos, each coming into the picture only to accomplish a specific task.

Just as a football team huddles to make sure everyone is aware of the goal and game plan, a true advisory team collaborates at the same table to make sure that everyone is clear about the strategies and expected outcomes. It becomes a process of breaking down silos and creating an environment for cohesive interaction.

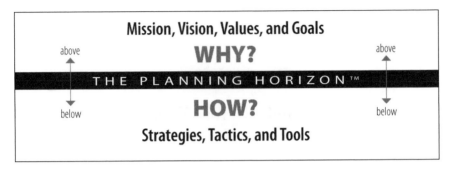

A true advisory team has many players—some who handle "above-the-line" activities (mission, vision, values, and goals) and others who handled "below-the-line" activities (strategies, tactics, and tools). The key to success is slotting the right advisors into the right spots.

The goal of this chapter is to help you evaluate the different advisors who could make up your team so that you—along with the help of a Wealth Coach—can choose the right team.

– WHO MAKES UP YOUR TEAM? —

Let's continue with the football analogy. Your role is the General Manager. One of your first tasks is to determine:

1. Who should be your "head coach"? For planning purposes, this person is called a Wealth Coach. The Wealth Coach will keep the overall strategy in mind and make sure that the right players are on the field at the right time.

2. Who are the starting players? These advisors will make up your Core Team, consisting of at least four people: a legal advisor, a tax advisor, a risk-management or insurance advisor, and an investment advisor. These people will be involved in most major decisions.

3. Finally, who are the specialized players? We call these players your Virtual Team because they have specific expertise that may be called upon from time to time to overcome obstacles—your kicker or your return man. These highly specialized team members step in to accompany you on a brief leg of your journey. A Virtual Team member might include a realtor, a business lawyer, or a mortgage broker, depending on your circumstances.

Before we talk about filling each of these slots, let's discuss how to evaluate advisors.

— EVALUATING THE ADVISOR —

The ideal advisor is someone who is invested in your success and, at the same time, is credible, reliable, and team-oriented—but finding all of those qualities in one person is rare. Fortunately, your advisors can do an exceptional job, even if they lack some of these qualities, as long as they are placed in the appropriate position.

David Maister, Charles Green, and Robert Galford, authors of *The Trusted Advisor* (Free Press, 2000), specified four criteria that help determine whether an advisor is a good fit for an available slot on a team.

Credibility: How much expertise and knowledge does your advisor have? A credible advisor makes you feel that you are in capable hands. An advisor who is credible will be skillful at "below-the-line" activities.

You will find that some of your advisors will do one task so well that you could not find a better resource for that specific knowledge. You might call these advisors Subject Matter Experts, and assign them to "below-the-line" activities. Other advisors might have a wide breadth of knowledge, so that they are able to understand your experts and integrate the totality of the planning recommendations into a tightly woven strategy that covers your situation perfectly. You might call these advisors Integrators. Both types of advisors can be very effective Core or Virtual Team members, but credibility alone is not sufficient to appoint someone as your Wealth Coach.

Reliability: Reliability means that you do not question your advisor's word. You know that he or she will follow through, and that the advisor says what he or she means and means what he or she says. Appointments are kept, paperwork is complete, research is thorough, and your information is accurate.

An advisor who is reliable will be great at "below-the-line" activities, but once again, reliability alone is not enough to assign this person to be your Wealth Coach.

Intimacy: Intimacy is all about the relationship you share with this person. Can you be completely open, or are you somewhat guarded? If you find yourself holding back, you are not going to be satisfied with the end results of your decision-making. If you feel that you can divulge your thoughts unabashedly, you have a high level of intimacy with this person. If you are concerned about revealing certain aspects of your personal business, your relationship will have a lower rating on the intimacy scale.

Intimacy often manifests as a gut feeling. Do you connect? Can you see that this advisor has empathy in the way he or she reacts to your comments and feelings?

An advisor with whom you connect will excel at "above-the-line" activities.

Self-Orientation: In this case, we want low self-orientation. Obviously, all advisors have a certain level of self-interest—they are exchanging services for income. However, consider the quality of your advisor's interest. Does your advisor care about delivering honest value, or is he or she going through the motions because he or she wants the paycheck?

An advisor with low self-orientation will excel at "above-the-line" activities.

— CHOOSING A WEALTH COACH —

Your Wealth Coach will help you appoint other team members, delegate responsibilities, and create a playbook. He or she will probably be the person who acts as your sounding board and helps you crystallize your vision. Most often, your Wealth Coach is someone with whom you have developed a trusted relationship.

Though a Wealth Coach does not necessarily need to be the most skilled in his or her chosen field, your Wealth Coach should be someone you trust to have your best interests in mind. Remember, this person will help you crystallize your vision. If you do not feel connected to an advisor, she or he can still sit on your team, but that advisor should not be your Wealth Coach.

To a large extent, assigning a Wealth Coach is based on your gut feeling. However, this position is critical, and gut feelings are often run by emotions. As such, your intuition should be complemented by logic. Consider that you should be able to answer *yes* to the following questions:

✓ Do I have good chemistry with my Wealth Coach?

✓ Is she or he a good listener?

✓ Does my Wealth Coach understand my core values and family history?

✓ Do I feel comfortable having a candid conversation with my Wealth Coach?

✓ Is he or she a natural leader, and will I trust him or her to take on the role of quarterback?

✓ Is the Wealth Coach a team player? Your Wealth Coach should be able to defer to those with more expertise, when appropriate. Your Wealth Coach should have a clear sense of when and how to get the best out of the planning team you assemble. A Wealth Coach confident in his or her abilities doesn't feel threatened when calling upon someone else with more direct knowledge. This is where the team approach offers a more well-rounded and comprehensive service. It is the best of both worlds.

Before appointing anyone as your Wealth Coach, be sure you are at peace with the answers to each of these questions. If the advisor passes the "gut check" test and is reliable, credible, and trustworthy, you have likely found your Wealth Coach and can begin looking for your Core Team members.

— CHOOSING A CORE TEAM —

Think of your Core Team members as your starting players—your quarterback, wide receiver, and running back. Your Core Team will be responsible for tax management, legal management, risk management, and investment management, meaning that it will consist of at least a tax-related professional, a lawyer, a risk-management/insurance professional, and an investment advisor. Typically, your Wealth Coach will fill one of these slots. In other words, your Core Team will include four people (other than you), one of whom is also your Wealth Coach.

Some clients might also need to add additional team members. For instance, someone who has a lot of real estate might have a real-estate agent or a mortgage broker on the Core Team. Most often, however, Virtual Team members will fill these roles.

Your Core Team will be at the table as you walk through the VISOR process (or a similar process for uncovering your goals). Whatever the process, remember that your team should spend more time identifying your vision than creating solutions, and it should understand the importance of a continual review.

An effective team member:

- Knows that he or she is a member of a team. If team members work in isolation, they risk being counterproductive.

- Knows his or her responsibilities. Perhaps more importantly, each knows what he or she is **not** responsible for, thereby deferring to other team members when appropriate.

- Knows who is calling the play and who designed the play. Ultimately, you are calling the play, but the Wealth Coach is second in command.

- Is accountable to a shared goal or goals. Without common goals, how does anyone know when his or her work, even one phase of it, is done?

Remember, too, that you must have team members who—collectively or as individuals—can work both "below" and "above the line."

"ABOVE-THE-LINE" ADVISORS

As we discussed in earlier chapters, you need to have clarity about your personal circumstances, goals, and desired outcome. This type of vision-setting requires advisors with whom you feel trusting enough to discuss delicate matters. Your Wealth Coach and at least one or two other Core Team members must be able to work "above the line." However, your Wealth Coach will have done most of the questioning process with you and your spouse in a more intimate and non-threatening session before other members are brought in to discuss your now clarified mission, vision, values, and goals. Clarity can be difficult to obtain, so be sure that you have Core Team members who shine when it comes time for the clarity-planning process.

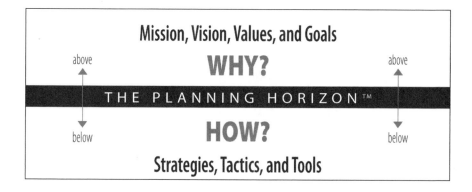

"BELOW-THE-LINE" ADVISORS

You must also have advisors who can work "below the line," particularly if you have sticky situations involving family members, second marriages, or complicated assets that require creative solutions.

Your Core Team must consist of at least two members who are expert implementers. "Below-the-line" advisors make sure that nothing falls through the cracks. They get the job done the way you want it done. You might not be particularly intimate with your "below-the-line" advisors, but they will be instrumental in executing your plan.

That said, it is often difficult to find advisors who excel both "above the line" and "below the line." However, it is necessary that all team members understand and respect the importance of the "above the line" and "below the line" issues. This is the power of a team. If one team member excels "below the line," he or she can hold accountable those team members who are great "above the line" but lack specific expertise in some "below the line" issues.

— CHOOSING A VIRTUAL TEAM—

Think of your Virtual Team as your kickers and return men. These are the people who step in to address one obstacle before moving on. These are the people who are occasionally copied on an email, but who are not always invited to the planning table.

Because Virtual Team members are, in essence, called in to design the solutions and file the papers, they must excel "below the line." There are no spots available for Virtual Team members who are not both reliable and competent.

Remember that not all Virtual Team members will be on the field at all times. Many clients have projects that necessitate drawing from different members of the Virtual Team at different times.

When Tom and Paula begin considering their team, they decide that Jennifer, their estate-planning lawyer, should be their Wealth Coach. Though Tom and Andrew, the financial advisor, had outstanding rapport, Jennifer excelled at both "above-the-line" and "below-the-line" activities from the beginning.

That said, Tom, Paula, and Jennifer know that Andrew will have an important role to play, and they definitely want Andrew at the table. This leaves two openings on the Core Team, to be filled by a tax professional and risk-management/insurance professional. Jennifer suggests that Tom and Paula also bring a business lawyer into the mix, at least for the time being. As Tom moves closer and closer to completing his initial goals of determining his Number and creating a Family Legacy, he will need to start giving serious thought to business-succession planning[8].

---

8 Wealth Coaches can have different core competencies in one or more of the following areas: investments, insurance, tax or legal. There is no advisor specialty that has the exclusive ability to fill this role.

— KEY POINTS —

> Creating the right advisory team has three steps:

> • It begins by identifying a Wealth Coach you trust, who excels "above the line," and with whom you have strong rapport. This person can help you appoint other team members, delegate responsibility, and create a playbook. Perhaps more importantly, your Wealth Coach will help you discover your vision and sustain your plan.

> • Once you have identified your Wealth Coach, you can begin filling the other slots with appropriate professionals. We call this the Core Team.

> Finally, appoint the Virtual Team. These are individuals with specific expertise who may be needed to help you address isolated events. Not all Virtual Team members will be on the field at all times. Many clients have multiple projects that necessitate drawing from different members of the Virtual Team at different times.

CHAPTER 8

Teamwork: Pulling in the Same Direction

Tom's son, Evan, is a little frustrated. His accountant mentioned that his estate would be subjected to a hefty estate tax upon his death. Although he may be comfortable now and able to live the lifestyle that he wants, the cash and investments that he has are not sufficient to pay estate-tax liability. He owns a few rental units that are paying nice rents, but the value of those units will create a tax that is far in excess of the resources he has to pay that tax. His accountant, Fiona, suggests that he speak to his insurance agent, Matthew. We call that the "hand-off."

Matthew suggests that Evan establish a mechanism that allows an influx of money upon his death so that his heirs can cover the estate-tax liabilities.

Matthew mentions that he has a terrific lawyer who can create this mechanism, as well as the other forms and procedures necessary to make such a technique work for Evan. Mitzi, the congenial lawyer, quotes Evan a fee that seems acceptable.

This second "hand-off" worked like a charm. Evan takes all the documents and forms back to his accountant, Fiona. He tells her that he followed her advice, but he is stopped cold by a frown on her face. Fiona explains to Evan that if he follows the lawyer's advice, Evan will end up paying substantial taxes this year.

What went wrong here?

First, unlike Tom's advisors, Evan's advisors worked in silos. They executed their agenda and not Evan's agenda. Substantial time and expense were wasted because they failed to communicate.

It is not uncommon for clients to attempt to plan, only to find that the people they hire to facilitate the planning are getting in the way. While most advisors do want what is best for their clients, they often have various approaches in arriving at "the best." These approaches are not always complementary. In this example, the approach that Matthew suggested did not complement the tax strategies that Fiona had already implemented.

This compartmentalized approach to planning is aggravated by two factors:

1. Most people are uncomfortable paying their advisors to have conversations. Imagine how you would feel if you were sent a bill every time one of your advisors communicates with another advisor. (Actually, you might be sent two bills, one from each advisor.) Your natural inclination might be to limit communication and cut to the chase.

2. Sometimes advisors do not want to collaborate with other advisors. These folks feel that they—and they alone—know best. Fortunately, if you followed our recommendations for deciding on the right planning team for you, these advisors will likely be weeded out.

In the last chapter, we made sure that you had the right team; in this chapter, we will take a look at how to manage your team so that it works together.

The scenario portrayed earlier cannot happen when you use the Planning Team Model. Your advisors cannot work in silos if you and your Wealth Coach are heading up a team effort. This chapter explains what this team effort looks like now that you have chosen your team members.

— THE TEAM'S GOALS —

In short, your team exists to:

1. <u>Manage the Discovery Process</u> – Do you have adequate clarity to make confident choices?

2. <u>Manage Gaps</u> – Are you tracking and managing the gap between your current status and your desired goals?

3. <u>Manage the Team</u> – Are you getting the most out of your resources?

4. <u>Manage Information</u> – Do team members have information when they need it and have they preserved it for future use?

5. <u>Manage Communication</u> – Are all the relevant players aware of all relevant team activities in a timely fashion?

6. <u>Manage Projects</u> – Are projects coordinated and managed in a timely and efficient manner?

7. <u>Manage Talent</u> – Is the right talent helping you at the right time?

8. <u>Manage Results</u> – Are your desired results achieved and maintained over time – thereby achieving sustainability?

FIRST MEETING

The most effective planning process seats you squarely at the head of the table. You have worked with one or more advisors to clarify your current situation and identify where you want your team to take you. Now it is time for you, the owner of the team, to make your needs and desires known through a "first meeting."

While this might seem like an expensive undertaking, we have found that a first meeting in which all advisors sit at a table and discuss the planning process is often the most important meeting that you can have. This meeting creates the groundwork and will ultimately save you time and money—after all, all of your team members will have an opportunity to coordinate, so the "hand off" is always appropriate. The result is that the time to complete the techniques you need to fill the gaps and realize your goals will be shortened, more effective and, ultimately, less costly.

In this first meeting, you must tell the team what you have been doing and what you expect from each of them. Planning for this meeting with your Wealth Coach is a must.

We suggest using an agenda. The three most important parts of the first meeting are:

1. **Operations:** How will the team operate? How frequently will the team meet? Will meetings be live or virtual? Which team members will attend which meetings? When will you be present?

   The answers to these questions will depend on the level of complexity and sophistication of your planning. More frequent meetings will be needed in direct relation to the complexity of the planning. In some cases, you will need meetings only once or twice a year, and in some cases you will need to meet more regularly. Be mindful that weekly meetings or teleconferences might be appropriate as a certain strategy, tactic, or tool is reviewed or implemented. The effective operation of the team will be dependent on the effective communication among all parties.

2. **Communications.** Led by the Wealth Coach, the team must then decide how it will communicate. How will it document decisions using a Planning Map (as discussed later in this chapter)? What will requests for additional research look like? How will deadlines be tracked?

   Be open to the team members' suggestions. After all, they may have participated in a number of planning-team situations, and their experiences might prove crucial in fashioning a method to complete your planning in the quickest and least painful way. Rely on your Wealth Coach to help shape the discussion and document the conclusions made during this most important planning meeting.

3. **Accountability.** You or your Wealth Coach must discuss the issue of accountability. Most of the time, the best way to create an accountable team is to require time commitments and establish the expectation that the Wealth Coach will monitor performance. Don't underestimate the power of peer pressure.

   All of your team members will want to present themselves to other advisors as competent and capable. The very act of publicly committing to a deadline will increase the probability that those commitments will be kept.

Your Wealth Coach should keep track of those commitments, and either you or the Wealth Coach should approach any team member who is constantly missing commitments. Be aware that not all advisors can work in a team setting. We believe this type of person will not produce the best results and should be replaced.

During this meeting, you should also be sure to discuss:

✓ Why you brought this group together.

✓ Your analysis of your current situation.

✓ The gaps that you perceive and the results you anticipate when those gaps are closed.

✓ Why you picked each of the advisors to work for your benefit, including the identification of the Wealth Coach as the overall coordinator of the team.

✓ Your expectations of the timing for work to be performed.

✓ What to do if conflicts become apparent.

✓ Budgeting. Based upon the foregoing explanations, request that all professionals who charge by time or task create a tentative budget for the work to be done. Ask them to break their estimates into phases, and demonstrate your understanding that phases might have to be budgeted when the exact techniques or planning actions are designed. The key here is to make sure that you communicate your expectations about billing. Advisors are not given carte blanche to try any and every strategy. They must stay focused, and you—the client—will be aware that when one phase ends, a new billing cycle will take effect.

✓ Finally, provide each advisor with license to communicate with each other, as long as that communication is judicious and productive.

The goals of the first meeting are to give the team members firm instructions, identify the players, and tell those players to play well together.

THE BIGGEST PROBLEM your team will face will be working with people who have such a strong disposition toward individualism that they are unable to consider other people's opinions. Having focused energy—even preferring to work alone—is fine, as long as the advisor can work well with a team. However, an advisor who has an "I-don't-care-what-you-think" attitude will jeopardize the integrity of the team. Regardless of whether they prefer to work alone, your team members must understand the strength of collaboration and cooperation. Two heads are better than one. An advisor who does not believe this will immediately make himself or herself known and must be removed from the team.

THE PLANNING MAP

Part of the first meeting will be a discussion of the "Planning Map," which will be used to document and manage all the moving pieces. A Planning Map is a checklist of sorts—a document created to identify and manage all the moving pieces. Without this tool, items might be overlooked and clients can risk losing focus on the important goals uncovered in the Discovery Phase.

A Planning Map can and should be customized based on a team or a client's preference. Some people are visual learners and need "mind maps." Other people prefer running checklists. Regardless of how you choose to organize your Planning Map, be sure it includes:

✓ Each action.

✓ What stage it is in (completed, deleted, in progress, rescheduled, scheduled, or tentative).

✓ A timeline.

✓ The team member responsible for completing the action.

The Planning Map not only outlines every item that needs to be addressed, but it also allows you to set a priority for each item. Perhaps the most important function of the Planning Map is that it outlines who is responsible for implementing certain tasks. When considering all the different players necessary to move a plan forward—estate planners, business lawyers, family lawyers, accountants, financial planners, insurance agents, and clients— you can imagine how important this resource can be.

The Planning Map becomes a living and breathing roadmap designed to ensure that the results you set out to achieve are not only implemented but also are sustained and constantly reviewed for relevance.

SAMPLE PLANNING MAP

JONES FAMILY PLANNING MAP FOR TOM AND PAULA JONES

PREPARED BY JENNIFER SMITH OF WEALTH COACH, INC.

THURSDAY, OCTOBER 27, 2011

Completed | Deleted | In Progress | Rescheduled | Scheduled | Tentative

| | 10/23/11 to 11/19/11 | 11/20/11 to 12/17/11 | 12/18/11 to 1/14/12 | 1/15/12 to 2/11/12 | 2/12/12 to 3/10/12 | 3/11/12 to 4/7/12 | 4/8/12 to 5/5/12 | 5/6/12 to 6/2/12 | 6/3/12 to 6/30/12 | 7/1/12 to 7/28/12 |

Discovery Profile
10/27/2011   11/24/2011
Clarify the mission, vision, values, and goals for Tom and Paula.

Financial Independence
11/16/2011   1/25/2012
Tom and Paula want to determine their financial independence need.

Business Succession
12/21/2011   4/18/2012
Tom needs to plan his exit from the business because this is his greatest asset to support financial independence.

Charitable Planning
2/15/2012   5/15/2012
Tom and Paula want to explore their philanthropic goals and determine what is possible once they have clarified their financial independence needs.

Estate Planning
2/15/2012   7/23/2012
Build Tom and Paula's comprehensive plan.

Family Legacy
3/6/2012   7/23/2012
Tom and Paula really want to create a structure for a family meeting to further discuss and document the family values and traditions.

Tom and Paula Jones (Initials) _____ / _____ Date

Copyright 2011 Legacy Wealth Coach Network™

Page 1 of 1

* Planning Map™ is a registered trademark of The Legacy Companies, LLC. All Rights Reserved.

MANAGING CONFLICT

Any process that stops feeling good usually has a breakdown in one of two areas:

1. You do not understand how the process works. Discussing these concerns as they surface can encourage your team to slow down and give you information as to why and how events are unfolding. In the areas of tax, insurance, and legal planning, strategies can be weighty and intricate, so you will likely encounter unfamiliar scenarios. Make sure your team explains all the steps and closes gaps in your knowledge so that you can move forward comfortably.

2. Your team might be going down the wrong track. If you intervene immediately, you can quickly review your goals and identify any misalignment so that the team can continue on course.

If you have that sinking feeling that your planning is not appropriate, you must immediately communicate that concern to your Wealth Coach and ultimately the team. Remember, they work for you.

— KEY POINTS —

❯ If your advisors are working in silos, they will likely take conflicting approaches to accomplishing your goals, which will waste time and money.

❯ Great approaches to achieving your mission, vision, values, and goals will be generated if the advisor team members are simultaneously connected to each other with the same information and are focused on the same issues.

❯ The Planning Team Model creates a coordinated team that exists to:

- Manage the Discovery Process

- Manage gaps

- Manage the team

- Manage information

- Manage communications

- Manage projects

- Manage talent

- Manage results

❯ The first meeting with your Planning Team is often the most important meeting that you can have. This meeting creates the groundwork and sets expectations for operations, communications, and accountability.

❯ Using a Planning Map will help synthesize efforts. A Planning Map is a document that identifies and manages all the moving pieces.

> If the planning process is not working, a breakdown probably exists in one of two areas:

  • You do not understand how the process works.

  • Your team might be going down the wrong track.

In either case, immediately communicate your concern to your Wealth Coach.

CHAPTER 9

Are You Really Done?

Tom, Paula, Jennifer, Andrew, and the rest of his team have accomplished a lot. They have found their Number, considered the Family Legacy, and discussed the couple's social legacy contributions. Although they know they still have a number of action items, almost all of Tom and Paula's original fears have been assuaged.

"When do you think we will be done?" Tom asks Jennifer.

Jennifer smiles sheepishly.

"Whenever I'm asked that question, I tell my clients that they are done when they can answer eight questions.

"Question #1: Does your plan meet and reflect your mission, vision, values, and goals?" she asks.

"Yes," says Tom.

"Question #2: Do you really understand your plan?"

Paula and Tom both nod. "We're two for two," says Tom.

"Question #3: Can you communicate the plan to the people you love?"

"I can," says Tom.

"So can I," says Jennifer.

"Question #4: Okay, then, the fourth question is this: *Have* you communicated the plan to the people you love?"

Tom nods, "We are halfway there."

Jennifer is still smiling as though she has something up her sleeve.

"Question #5: Does your plan accomplish what you want it to accomplish, when you want it to, for whom, and the way you want?" she asks.

"Yes, and that question is actually four questions," Tom teases.

"I just have three more," says Jennifer. **"Question #6: Do you have a trusted-advisor relationship with someone with whom you feel comfortable sharing anything?"**

"Yes," says Tom. "And did we tell you that we think you are a gem?"

"Well, thank you," says Jennifer, continuing her interrogation.

"Question #7: Do you meet with and hear from your advisors on a regular basis."

"You are on my speed dial," says Tom, with a nod.

"Okay, final question. Question #8: Are you sure that nothing is ever going to change in your life or in the world around you?"

Paula laughs.

"You got me," says Tom.

"That's right," says Jennifer. "Your life and the world around you are constantly changing. You achieve goals, set new ones, and change courses due to unforeseen circumstances. So your planning is never really done."

Planning truly is never really done. You might accomplish all of your original goals, but you will still want to get together with your planning group at least annually to discuss what has transpired since your last review. This is where we enter the fourth phase of the Wealth Optimization

System. Up until now, this book has explored your plan by working through a problem-solving process that directed you, first, to reach clarity about who you are and what you want to accomplish for yourself, your family, and your community (Phase One). Next, you learned how to work closely with a specialist who can design (Phase Two) and implement (Phase Three) strategies, tactics, and tools that assist you in accomplishing your financial, legacy, and community goals.

What if your planning efforts stopped here? What if you and your advisors did not meet for 10 or 20 years? You would be unable to change courses if the strategies stopped being relevant (or stopped working). This would be akin to having a pacemaker but never bothering to check to see if the battery is still working to keep your ticker ticking properly!

Instead, Phase Four (sustainability) helps you address these questions:

1. Have the eventual goals the group set out to achieve been met?

2. What is working?

3. If successful, what are the specific and measurable outcomes that indicate success?

4. How does the desired outcome (clarity) relate to the present situation (result of implementation)?

5. What is not working?

6. Has the goal changed? Seeing that your planning continues to be relevant and viable is so important to a sustained and ever more productive planning on your part. This invariably will lead you and your advisors back into a conversation about your having continued clarity around your mission, vision, values, and goals (Discovery).

The truth of the matter is this: No matter how thorough your planning activities are, your life will inevitably change, which will require your plan to change as well.

Anything that lies stagnant will eventually become stale or deteriorate.

In the worst-case scenario, it will decay and even become dangerous. Consider buying a vacation home that sits unused for ten years. You do not even hire a caretaker to attend to it. Would it maintain its usefulness when you revisit it?

Most people consider planning to be an isolated one-time action. This attitude places too little attention on the fact that there must be a mechanism to make sure a plan works over the lifetime of the stated intentions. Remember that your vision evolves, people change, laws are updated, and financial markets shift.

We counsel our clients to focus on Ultimate Ends rather than Intermediate Ends. What is the difference? **Ultimate Ends** focus on the long-term results. **Intermediate Ends** focus on the planning mechanisms.

When creating their estate plan, Tom and Paula want to make sure that their children and grandchild have enough money to be cared for, but not enough that they become spendthrifts. They can either focus on stringent trust language that protects their children and grandson from the spoils of excess wealth or they can focus on creating mechanisms that teach their children that money is simply a tool to be used with care and training. Though creating stringent trust language (the Intermediate Ends) might be a good idea, Tom and Paula should focus on teaching the children how to use money wisely—the Ultimate Ends.

One of our primary goals in writing this book is to provide you with a framework for making planning decisions that honor your Ultimate Ends. A second goal is to teach you the importance of managing and sustaining the plan.

Anything that is put in place with the hopes for long-term results requires sustainability. Once a strategy is set in motion, it requires diligence to keep it current, viable, and relevant.

- Your plan is kept **current** if you consider your family's emotional state, financial security, and demographics.

- Your plan is **viable** if it has been adjusted in accordance with tax, probate, trust, and other laws, as well as with the state of the economy and the financial markets.

- For a plan to continue to be **relevant**, it must continue to support your broader vision—your Ultimate Ends, which might change over time.

Your initial efforts—engaging in a detailed Discovery Process, evaluating and deciding upon which creative strategies will help you achieve what you want, and implementing those strategies—do provide a great deal of assurance that you will create your own unique journey. However, just as an airplane pilot must continuously adjust his plane's flight path (due to the impact of wind, storms, other traffic) to arrive at the desired destination, you and your advisory team must be willing to engage in a formalized approach that challenges all involved to make sure that the current strategies remain viable and relevant to sustain your plan.

Tom looks at Jennifer a little sheepishly.

"So I guess we aren't going to be done any time soon."

Jennifer slides a copy of Tom and Paula's Planning Map across the table.

The Planning Map includes several items, which the team is only beginning to address, such as business-succession planning, the couple's philanthropic goals, family meetings and briefings, and official documentation of family experiences, values, and traditions.

Tom is especially anxious to begin determining how he will transition out of business, the next highest priority.

"I know I'm giving you a hard time about wrapping this up," Tom says, "but the truth is that I really like this process. How did you get to be so good at your job?"

TOM & PAULA'S PLANNING MAP

JONES FAMILY PLANNING MAP FOR TOM AND PAULA JONES

PREPARED BY JENNIFER SMITH OF WEALTH COACH, INC.

THURSDAY, OCTOBER 27, 2011

Legend: Completed · Deleted · In Progress · Rescheduled · Scheduled · Tentative

	10/23/11 to 11/19/11	11/20/11 to 12/17/11	12/18/11 to 1/14/12	1/15/12 to 2/11/12	2/12/12 to 3/10/12	3/11/12 to 4/7/12	4/8/12 to 5/5/12	5/6/12 to 6/2/12	6/3/12 to 6/30/12	7/1/12 to 7/28/12

Discovery Profile
10/27/2011 — 11/24/2011
Clarify the mission, vision, values, and goals for Tom and Paula.

Financial Independence
11/16/2011 — 1/25/2012
Tom and Paula want to determine their financial independence need.

Business Succession
12/21/2011 — 4/18/2012
Tom needs to plan his exit from the business because this is his greatest asset to support financial independence.

Charitable Planning
2/15/2012 — 5/15/2012
Tom and Paula want to explore their philanthropic goals and determine what is possible once they have clarified their financial independence needs.

Estate Planning
2/15/2012 — 7/23/2012
Build Tom and Paula's comprehensive plan.

Family Legacy
3/6/2012 — 7/23/2012
Tom and Paula really want to create a structure for a family meeting to further discuss and document the family values and traditions.

Tom and Paula Jones (Initials) _____ / _____ Date

Page 1 of 1

"I owe that to the Legacy Wealth Coach Network," she says. Jennifer explains that the Legacy Wealth Coach Network is a group of financial professionals from the United States and Canada who share best practices, such as the Wealth Optimization System and VISOR.

"Well, I've got a message for the Legacy Wealth Coach Network," says Tom.

"What's that?" asks Jennifer.

"Tell them I can finally sleep soundly."

— KEY POINTS —

> Because your vision evolves, people change, laws are updated, and financial markets shift, your plan must be sustained and managed. Anything that is put in place with the hopes for long-term results requires sustainability. Once a strategy is set in motion, it requires diligence to keep it current, viable, and relevant.

> To keep your plan current, viable, and relevant, be sure to meet with your team to answer these six questions:

  1. Have the eventual goals been met?

  2. What is working?

  3. What are the specific and measurable outcomes that determine success (or lack thereof)?

  4. How does the original desired outcome related to the present situation?

  5. What is not working?

  6. Has the goal been changed?

> We counsel our clients to focus on Ultimate Ends rather than Intermediate Ends. When managing your plan, focus on the long-term results rather than the planning mechanism. If a planning mechanism (Intermediate Ends) is not reaching a long-term goal (Ultimate Ends), or if the long-term goal has changed, the planning mechanism must change.

> A plan must be kept current, relevant, and viable.

   • Your plan is kept **current** if you consider your family's emotional state, financial security, and demographics.

- Your plan is **viable** if it has been adjusted in accordance with tax, probate, trust, and other laws, as well as the state of the economy and the financial markets.

- Your plan is **relevant** if it continues to support your broader vision—your Ultimate Ends, which might change over time.

Planning is fun. Yes, you read that right. I wrote **fun**.

Now, I know that clients don't usually look forward to the planning process. Certainly, they want to spend as little time as possible (and as little money as possible) dealing with documents, strategies, taxes, business structures, estate plans, and other complexities.

If the process is organized by the right team and headed by a Wealth Coach, planning is exciting because it leads to desirable results for the client, his or her loved ones, the community, and the philanthropic causes about which the client is passionate.

This is why planning is fun. With each new strategy, a client is able to anticipate and eagerly await the positive consequences.

It is my hope that this book has created a blueprint for you to create and find the right team. As you search for the right Wealth Coach and Core Team members, remember to use the Legacy Wealth Coach Network™ as a resource.

The Legacy Wealth Coach Network stretches from coast-to-coast throughout North America. The network is a professional association of highly accomplished, multi-disciplinary professionals who are successfully using the approaches outlined in these chapters to help individuals, families, and businesses alike fulfill their dreams. Its members are ready and willing to assist you and your current advisory team in a number of capacities.

The authors of this book represent nineteen member firms of The Legacy Wealth Coach Network, and I would like to introduce you to them. Together, they bring more than 600 years of experience advising clients and providing clarity where life intersects wealth.

William A. Barill, CFP®, CLU, ChFC

Legacy Wealth Coach™

Sarnia, Ontario & London, Ontario

Bill is the tax- and estate-planning partner with Barill and Company, a family firm working with privately held businesses throughout southwestern Ontario, with offices in London and Sarnia. Over three decades, his company has evolved, developing a business model to support comprehensive planning for private corporations, their owners, and their clients. The unique process of the legacy system is an important component in Barrill and Company's comprehensive planning for business owners, which includes succession and exit strategies, benefits and pension-plan design, as well as financial independence and wealth optimization planning.

Daniel Barill

Legacy Wealth Coach™

Sarnia, Ontario & London, Ontario

After several private- and public-enterprise experiences, Dan joined a successful and evolving family financial-services firm, Barill and Company. He has developed a model that transforms entrepreneurs' business success into personal wealth for themselves and the communities in which they are involved. A devotee of the Legacy Wealth Coach Network philosophy, Dan believes that his unique approach has resulted in the clarity and happiness his clients have experienced. This perspective has contributed to Barill and Company's identity as a recognized choice for family business in southern Ontario.

Mayur T. Dalal, MBA

Legacy Wealth Coach™
Lake Success, New York

Mayur is the founder and CEO of The Oxford Group of Lake Success, located in Lake Success, New York. The focus of the firm is to help clients gain clarity around their core values and to reflect these in their life- and wealth-coaching plans. For over 22 years, Mayur has worked with high-net-worth clients, initially focusing on insurance, estate planning, and investment strategies, and then expanding into an expanded advisory and advocacy role for families, family offices, and businesses. Mayur is a charter member of the Boston-based Legacy Wealth Coach Network, and he employs the unique process developed by the Network to ensure that his clients achieve clarity, simplicity, and peace of mind when managing their wealth. Mayur is a graduate of the Mumbai University in India.

John M. Dankovich, J.D., CLU, ChFC

Legacy Wealth Coach™
Auburn Hills, Michigan

John is one of the founding partners at MKD Wealth Coaches, a wealth-coaching company in Auburn Hills, Michigan. His work stands as a testament to the corporate mission, "helping people experience abundant life." John is passionate about listening to the heart of each of his clients; his strength lies in formulating personalized strategies to surround and achieve their revealed desires. John has taken this approach successfully for the past 25 years, and his connection with The Legacy Wealth Coach Network has further solidified his beliefs in values-based planning. As a Wealth Coach, he is defined by his ability to help others achieve their financial goals. In his role as an advisor, John has built personal relationships that mirror those of family, friend, and mentor. His work substantiates the inherent importance of relationships in achieving goals.

Chuck Ebersole, CLU, ChFC, CFP®

Legacy Wealth Coach™
Sacramento, California

Chuck is a partner of the financial advisory firm of Foord, Van Bruggen, Ebersole, & Pajak in Sacramento, California; he is the author of *The Value of "Beyond Expectations" Service* and co-author of *It's Not About Your Money, It's About Your Life.* Since 1974, he has advised individuals and families as they navigate through the complexities of financial and estate planning to achieve their goals and dreams. His passion for helping clients who struggle to complete their planning is unmatched. His process allows clients to achieve clarity about their mission, vision, values, and goals; it eliminates conventional struggles, and creates truly meaningful and sustainable plans. The process has propelled clients to high levels of satisfaction for both themselves and their families. Chuck credits the following belief as the key to his clients' impressive rate of success: "When you focus on what is important to you, maintaining it for yourself, your loved ones, and your legacy becomes mandatory."

W. Duke Grkovic, CFP®, MSFS
Legacy Wealth Coach™
Richmond, Virginia
Duke is founder and president of Cambridge Advisors, located in Richmond, Virginia. Duke has a degree from Cornell University, and a master's degree in financial services; he is a certified financial planner and a chartered life underwriter. These excellent credentials go only so far in explaining the wealth of assets he and his team bring to their clients. As important as expertise and 30-plus years of experience are, it is Duke's special perspective that matters most: "I realized well into my own professional journey that many clients who were growing in wealth were not necessarily growing in personal satisfaction. I thought we could help. We've gone beyond the traditional wealth-management model. We look at the whole person, because true net worth cannot be measured in dollars alone."

Denice (Denny) Gustin-Piazza, CFP®, CFS, CRC
Legacy Wealth Coach™
Des Plaines, Illinois
Denny is the president and founder of WealthPlanners, LLC in Des Plaines, Illinois, a collaborative wealth-management firm which serves the diverse needs of business owners and professionals. Committed to innovation and excellence in planning, she has worked with a number of women's organizations and charitable organizations. In 2002, Denny co-authored the book

Winning Financial Strategies for Women. Her warmth, understanding, and positive outlook have helped her to build deep and lasting relationships as she supports clients through the transitions, crises, and opportunities that life brings.

Scott D.C. Harris, CSA, CLU, CFP®
Legacy Wealth Coach™
Toronto, Ontario
Scott is a Wealth & Estate Planning Advisor and co-founder of Toronto, Ontario-based Stonehaven Financial Group, a boutique planning firm that uses a disciplined process to help clients explore the relationship between life and money. With over 15 years of experience collaborating with top entrepreneurs and professionals from across Canada, he works with his clients to grow and secure their wealth by helping them to take action on their advantages.

Thomas P. Holland, CFP®
Legacy Wealth Coach™
Norwell, Massachusetts
Tom is a founding partner of the wealth-advisory firm of Global Vision Advisors in Norwell, Massachusetts. Global Vision Advisors provides individuals and families with sophisticated financial counsel. Tom's firm is unique in its ability to deliver comprehensive and high-quality money management and insurance solutions normally associated with larger firms in a more client-centered and modern approach. Prior to forming Global Vision Advisors, Tom was a partner with Scott Fithian in a wealth-advisory practice, and he contributed to Todd and Scott's efforts to create and deliver content to the Legacy Wealth Coach Network.

Scott R. Lebin, RFC
Legacy Wealth Coach™
Geneva, Illinois
Scott is the founder of Managed Economics for Doctors, Inc., and Lebin Financial Planning in Geneva, Illinois. He has worked exclusively with high-net-worth individuals for 26 years and has extensive experience in investment management, retirement, and estate planning, with special

focus on medical professionals. Scott works with wealthy families and has authored articles about managed economics in *M.D. News Magazine*. Scott helps clients maximize capital accumulation while protecting and preserving their assets. He has presented motivational seminars throughout the United States. He has been Chairman of the Board of the Geneva Chamber of Commerce for over 13 years. He is trustee and Chair of the Governance committee of Upper Iowa University and serves as a committee member of the Million Dollar Round Table. He is also President of the TFA Circle of Honor Society. He received the Wood Award, citizen of the year recognition, in 2008, from Geneva, Illinois.

Lawrence M. Lehmann, J.D.

Legacy Wealth Coach™
New Orleans, Louisiana

Larry practices law as a Louisiana board-certified specialist in estate planning and administration and taxation at the firm of Lehmann Norman & Marcus LC. He has served as president of the Greater New Orleans Council of the Partnership for Philanthropic Planning, the Jewish Children's Regional Service, the New Orleans Hillel Foundation, and the New Orleans Friends of Music. He currently serves as a member of the Board of Directors of the National Association of Estate Planners and Councils, and is a member of the Legacy Wealth Coach Network. In addition, Larry is an instrument-rated pilot and is a founding member of Pilots for Patients, a non-profit organization that provides air transportation for patients who require specialized medical care at distant healthcare facilities.

Allison Maher, CA, CFP®, TEP

Legacy Wealth Coach™
Calgary, Alberta

Allison is the co-founder of Family Wealth Coach Planning Services, a Canadian firm based in Calgary, Alberta. Over the past 15 years, she has become the "Chief Legacy Officer" for many Canadian families and uses the Legacy Wealth Optimization System™ as a touchstone in all her work. As a family Wealth Coach, she specializes in working with multi-generational family offices and high-net-worth individuals, with a focus on insurance and succession planning. Allison is a chartered accountant, a certified financial planner, and a member of the Society of Trust and Estate Practitioners. She was recognized as one of Calgary's "Top 40 under 40" in *Avenue Magazine* (2009).

Patrick O'Connor, CFP®, CLU, ChFC, TEP

Legacy Wealth Coach™
Winnipeg, Manitoba

Pat is a founder and president of Blackwood Wealth Planning based in Winnipeg, Manitoba. Over the past ten years, Pat has focused on using the disciplined planning approach of the Legacy Wealth Coach Network as the foundation for his business. This disciplined approach that is driven by his clients' values has proven to be an effective process to deal with the many complex issues which affluent families face.

Ed Postrozny, CFP®, CLU, ChFC

Legacy Wealth Coach™
Toronto, Ontario

Based in Toronto, Ontario, Ed is the founder and principal of Postrozny Financial Security, Inc. His company specializes in working with business owners, professionals, and their advisors. It is not unusual for his company to have as many as three generations of the same family in different stages of planning. Legacy planning is a key aspect of the work done with clients, helping them to meet their personal and business objectives. As continuity and sustainability are key components of every plan, Ed has developed the business and its succession to ensure his clients every opportunity for continued success. Ed feels privileged for the opportunity to work with his daughter Dana and have her as part of his succession plan.

Tony A. Rose, C.P.A.

Legacy Wealth Coach™
Los Angeles, California & Las Vegas, Nevada

Tony is a founding partner of the CPA firm of Rose, Snyder & Jacobs in Los Angeles; principal of RSJ/Swenson, a management and human-resources consulting firm with offices in Los Angeles and Las Vegas; and author of *Say Hello to the Elephants*. Since 1976, his CPA firm has provided tax and management consulting advice to closely held corporations, family-owned businesses, partnerships, and the high-net-worth individuals who own them. Through counseling and leading multi-disciplinary teams of professionals, Tony has provided valuable guidance in resolving the complexities faced by families of wealth.

Tom Sorge CLU, ChFC, CFP®, TEP

Legacy Wealth Coach™
Calgary, Alberta

Tom is a co-founder of Family Wealth Coach Planning Services, a Canadian firm based in Calgary, Alberta. Over the past 30 years, he has worked with many businesses and families on financial and estate-planning issues, using the Legacy Wealth Optimization System™ exclusively. As a family Wealth Coach, he specializes in working with multi-generational family offices and high-net-worth individuals, with a focus on insurance and succession planning. Tom is a chartered life underwriter, certified financial planner, and a member of the Society of Trust and Estate Practitioners.

Frank Spezzano CLU, ChFC, MSFS, AEP

Legacy Wealth Coach™
Philadelphia, Pennsylvania

Frank is the founder of IRUS Advisory in Philadelphia, Pennsylvania. Since 1985, he has been engaged as the trusted advisor and financial concierge for clients throughout the country. Frank and the IRUS staff assist their clientele in handling, positioning, and monitoring their financial holdings, investments, business transactions, and various other legal and financial affairs. Of particular mention is the success which the IRUS clients have had in transitioning their business interests to the next generation and to outside investors.

Robert Taylor, CFP®, CLU, ChFC

Legacy Wealth Coach™
Vancouver, British Columbia

Rob is a partner and director of TRG Group Benefits, a Canadian firm based in Vancouver, British Columbia. Rob's firm focuses specifically on the management and delivery of sustainable benefit programs. TRG has had the most success with organizations that are committed to exploring the full potential of the relationship they seek with their employees. With the constant pressures of healthcare inflation, TRG's expertise has never been more impactful in the navigation through this complexity. It starts with understanding and helping organizations articulate their values and carrying this message to their people. Expressing care for their employees is paramount, and TRG provides significant resources and support to illustrate this care through the delivery of world-class benefit programs. Rob's 23 years of experience contribute to TRG's more than 300 years of advisor expertise.

Julianne (Julie) Thornton, CFP®
Legacy Wealth Coach™
Des Plaines, Illinois

Julie is a partner with WealthPlanners, LLC, a collaborative wealth-management firm in Des Plaines, Illinois, which is dedicated to helping business owners and professionals articulate their vision, define their objectives, and discern optimal strategies for their lifestyle and wealth. A seasoned industry veteran and two-time cancer survivor, Julie's insights gained from her personal journey have enabled her to guide her clients through the challenges, transitions, and complexities of their own lives with skill and compassion.

— AN INVITATION TO CONNECT —

If you're interested in locating a Legacy Wealth Coach to assist yourself, your family or your business through the process outlined in this book, you can contact The Legacy Companies, LLC at 888-649-4591 or email: wealthcoach@legacyboston.com.

— ADVISORS —

If you're an advisor interested in becoming a Legacy Wealth Coach and learning more about the model outlined in this book, you can contact The Legacy Companies, LLC, at 888-649-4591 or visit the www.legacyboston.com to learn more.